Running
SNOB

Running SNOB

Kevin Nelson

Guilford, Connecticut

An imprint of Globe Pequot

Distributed by NATIONAL BOOK NETWORK

Copyright © 2017 by Kevin Nelson

Illustrations by Meredith Nelson

British Library Cataloguing in Publication Information Available

Library of Congress Cataloging-in-Publication Data Available

ISBN 978-1-4930-2624-1
ISBN 978-1-4930-2625-8 (e-book)

♾™ The paper used in this publication meets the minimum requirements of American National Standard for Information Sciences—Permanence of Paper for Printed Library Materials, ANSI/NISO Z39.48-1992.

Printed in the United States of America

Be smart, have fun, live life with flair.

—The Snob's maxim

CONTENTS

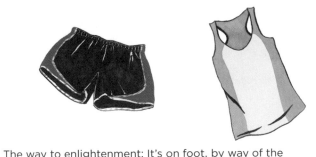

INTRODUCTION

Marathoner Rachel Toor delightfully confesses to something that many runners may think privately but few would dare say publicly. "I'm a runner," she says. "Not only that, I'm a snob, if being a snob means that I value excellence."

Jeff Galloway, the popular marathon coach and a former Olympian in the 10,000 meters, is the last person one would accuse of being a snob. His coaching philosophy is centered on the idea that anyone with the courage to start a marathon has the ability to finish it, even, as he puts it, "former couch potatoes."

And once they do, once they cover those hallowed 26.2 miles, those one-time couch potatoes enter into an elite realm, in Galloway's view. "To reach the finish line in a marathon is to enter an elite group; only about one-tenth of 1 percent of the population does it," he says.

Now, let's imagine a marathon in progress—New York. Mile 4, Fourth Avenue, Brooklyn. Some runners—first-timers, all seeking to join those elite ranks Galloway refers to—suddenly stop running and start walking. They walk for a while and then start running again, taking another walk break a few miles later. They do this throughout the race, and they do it all the way to Central Park—walking and running, following the methods that Galloway teaches on how first-timers can finish a marathon.

As these first-timers exult in triumph, other runners, battle-hardened veterans of the sport, are not so pleased. One of them is acclaimed Japanese writer and novelist Haruki Murakami, a veteran of New York and other marathons, as well as the 62-mile Lake Saroma Ultramarathon in his homeland. While supporting the idea of people exercising

more and getting into better shape, Murakami feels strongly that if you walk during a marathon, it puts you into a different and lesser category than someone who runs through Mile 4 and all the other miles. Yes, you have covered the distance around the five boroughs and good for you, but you have not *run* it. Murakami claims to have never walked during a marathon and vows he never will.

Three runners, all different. Yet each of them has views that can be characterized as snobbish or elitist. But they are merely expressing their own personal standards and values, and those standards and values help them form judgments and have opinions and provide the foundation upon which they live their lives. What's wrong with that?

Plenty, if you ask Hollywood. Look at *McFarland USA*, the 2015 Disney movie based on a true story about a Central Valley high school cross-country coach (played by Kevin Costner) whose underdog team of Hispanic runners overcomes the long odds against them and wins the California state championship. Naturally the teams they beat are composed of snobs—snotty, vaguely sinister prep school boys. If Draco Malfoy had gone out for track, he would've been running against McFarland.

Although many of those who make and star in movies live in gated enclaves in Beverly Hills, earn six-figure incomes, and send their children to the best private schools, you see this same basic script over and over. Need a villain? Cut to the snob, the elitist, the person of privilege. Snobs look down their noses at outsiders, the others, those who do not belong to their clique.

The most popular running movie ever made, *Chariots of Fire*—whose theme song is, to borrow Steve Dollar's phrase, the ultimate ear worm; once you hear it, it burrows into your brain to take up permanent residence—follows this standard theme, even though its two

main characters attend Cambridge University, which is not exactly, you know, McFarland High. One of the characters (based on the real-life Eric Liddell) is Scottish and champions Scottish independence as well as his devout Christian beliefs, while the other main character (also based on a real person, Harold Abrahams—both he and Liddell won gold medals in the sprints in the 1924 Summer Olympics)—is Jewish and refuses to buckle under to the anti-Jewish attitudes and actions of Cambridge authorities. Standing in the way of both men are upper-crust English snobs (one of whom is wonderfully played by Sir John Gielgud, who was probably a snob in real life and proud of it).

Ironically, given that both these movies are about running, many people regard running itself as an elite activity. Indeed it is. The Harold Abrahams–Eric Liddell of our time is the charismatic and gregarious Jamaican sprinter Usain St. Leo Bolt. He has a box full of gold medals and has run the 100 meters in 9.58 seconds and the 200 meters in 19.19 seconds, both world records. That, my friends, is as elite as it gets.

There's nothing wrong with being an elite, in our view, as long as you have a good time and a sense of humor about it, like the dashing, smiling, posing, high-strutting Mr. Bolt. That's our goal here at *Running Snob* too. Flip back to our table of contents page and you'll see what we're up to: stories and anecdotes, humor, satire, informative lists aplenty, entertaining trivia, tips and advice, inspirational quotations, interactive quizzes and games, and lots of stuff about the grand races and personalities—Joan Benoit Samuelson, Meb Keflezighi, Fred Lebow, Paula Radcliffe, Steve Prefontaine, Galen Rupp, Bill Rodgers, Des Linden, Frank Shorter, Neanderthal Man, and Forrest Gump—of the sport.

Runners aren't better than everyone else. They are for the most part in better shape, though. Let's have some fun.

—Kevin Nelson

CHAPTER ONE

The Community of Running

Forget all that "loneliness of the long distance runner" stuff. Running isn't lonely anymore, at least not as lonely as it used to be. Running is community and family. It is clubs, groups, teams. It is people coming together to have fun and financially support other people who may need their help. These and other topics are explored in this chapter.

RUNNING IS THE BEST.

IT'S THE UNIVERSAL SPORT.

BUT WHY?

Next to walking, running is the world's most popular form of exercise. Millions of people enter races every year, and billions more do it every day without going near a formal competition. Why is running so popular? Some thoughts:

IT IS AS HUMAN AS EATING OR SLEEPING.

Virtually everyone has felt the joy of putting one foot in front of the other and running. No need for lots of money or specialized gear. Many runners even reject shoes. And all who do it, certainly when they are young, derive pleasure from the act.

RUNNING CRASHES BOUNDARIES.

It is open and freely available to all cultures, races, ethnicities, religions, and nationalities. Look at the last names of these top distance runners of recent times: Keflezighi, Goucher, Ritzenhein, Kastor, Rupp, Flanagan, Puskedra, Kibet, Khannouchi. And these are just the Americans.

RUNNING IS GLOBAL.

The best sprinters today are Jamaicans and Americans. The best distance runners are Kenyans and Ethiopians. Every year the six top

marathons occur in six global capitals—Boston, Chicago, New York, Berlin, London, Tokyo—in four countries on three continents.

RUNNING IS A SHARED EXPERIENCE.

The woman who steps out for a run along the canal streets of Amsterdam shares the same fundamental experience as a trail runner in the Blue Ridge Mountains above Asheville, a group of college students at a meet-up for an easy 5- to 10-miler in the early morning darkness of Austin's Town Lake Trail, or a San Jose day trader who gets up early to walk and jog before the markets open back East and he must go to work. It's all running.

BOTH MEN AND WOMEN RUN, AND BOTH EXCEL AT IT.

Not only that, men who later become women also run, and one of them was truly exceptional at it. This was Bruce Jenner, now Caitlyn Jenner, who won the gold medal for the decathlon in the 1976 Montreal Olympic Games. Jenner famously waved a little American flag in celebration after crossing the finish of the 1,500 meters, the final event of the decathlon.

MIDDLE-AGED AND OLDER PEOPLE RUN, AND THEY ALSO EXCEL AT IT.

There are countless stories, now a commonplace, of older sedentary adults who, hoping to lose weight or break a smoking habit or reinvent

SNOB ASIDE

How do human runners compare to animals? Animals go faster over shorter distances. The pronghorn antelope, gazelle, and wildebeest can reach speeds up to 60 mph in a sprint. The cheetah, the Flash of the animal kingdom, beats them by a nose; its fastest recorded time is 61 mph. Usain Bolt's world record of 9.58 seconds for the 100 meters translates to about 28 mph.

themselves in some way, take up running and transform their lives. Many of these same people post frequent updates on their exploits on Facebook, getting likes from some and groans from others.

PEOPLE OF ALL SHAPES AND SIZES RUN.
Paula Radcliffe, the great British champion, has the ideal runner's body—long and lean and super fit with legs that gobble up the asphalt. But there are all types of bodies in running, all shapes and sizes, some hard and chiseled and others soft as an overripe banana. It's an activity that permits ordinary people to do extraordinary things.

PEOPLE WITH INCREDIBLE PHYSICAL AND EMOTIONAL CHALLENGES DO IT, PEOPLE LIKE BEN BALTZ.
Ben Baltz of Valparaiso, Florida, contracted bone cancer at age six, and doctors surgically removed his lower right leg to stop the disease from spreading. After being fitted with a prosthetic leg, on a walk with his mother one day he realized he could do more than walk, he could run. One year after surgery he ran the mile in a little over eight minutes. Now in his teens, he runs races, does triathlons, and has his sights set on finishing a marathon.

HOLLYWOOD ACTION STARS DO IT.
While their stories hardly compare to Ben's, every action star uses running in his movies as a way to convey vigor, vitality, and physicality. Virtually every action movie ever made in the history of action movies contains at least one scene of the star sprinting somewhere at a furious pace. A classic sequence might consist of a Daniel Craig or Tom Cruise screeching up in his car (for Craig it would be an Aston, of course), jumping out, and firing off a round of gunfire at the bad guy he's chasing, then taking off on foot to try to nab him.

MANY SMART, HARD-WORKING PEOPLE DRAW SUSTENANCE FROM IT.

In the film *The Imitation Game,* Benedict Cumberbatch plays Alan Turing, the genius Cambridge mathematician who invented a machine that cracked the Nazi Enigma code during World War II and prefigured the modern development of computers. The movie shows scenes of Cumberbatch running, a nod to Turing who was, in fact, a long-distance runner in real life. He ran in school as a boy and, like so many others seeking to alleviate stress and get into better health, he returned to it as an adult. "I have such a stressful job that the only way I can get it out of my mind is by running hard," Turing told a friend once. "It's the only way I can get some release."

WILLIAM SHAKESPEARE WAS A RUNNER.

Solitary, introspective, thoughtful, William Shakespeare had the mind of a poet—and a runner. He surely walked places as a man and ran as a boy. A few lines from his plays even seem to resonate across the centuries to runners today:

"Now bid me run, and I will strive with things impossible."

—*Julius Caesar*, Act 2, Scene 1

"I see you stand like greyhounds in the slips, straining upon the start."

—*Henry V*, Act 3, Scene 1 (the hunt he describes also evokes the mood at the start of a footrace)

"Wisely and slow; they stumble that run fast."

—*Romeo and Juliet*, Act 2, Scene 3

"A merry heart goes all day."

—*The Winter's Tale*, Act 4, Scene 3

5

FORREST GUMP WAS A RUNNER TOO.

Determined, driven, purposeful, Forrest Gump had the mind of a runner too. The gift of running freed him from a disability as a child, and as a private in the US Army it helped him carry his wounded comrades to safety in a Vietnam firefight. Later he became an ultramarathoner. A few thoughts from him on his favorite activity:

- "You wouldn't believe it if I told you I can run like the wind. From that day on, if I was going somewhere, I was running." —*on how he became a runner*
- "It used to be I ran to get me where I was going. I never thought it would take me anywhere."
- "That day, for no particular reason, I decided to go for a run. For no particular reason, I just kept on going."
- "They just couldn't believe somebody would do all that running for no particular reason. I just felt like running." —*on why he ran for three years straight, back and forth across America*
- "My momma always said there's an awful lot you can tell about a person by his shoes. Where they goin', where they been."

FROM NEANDERTHAL MAN TO TODAY

THE AGES OF RUNNING EVOLUTION

Running is one of Man's oldest activities, and its evolution can be summed up in four distinct historical epochs. Here are four archetypal runners from those eras, extending from prehistoric times to today.

NEANDERTHAL MAN, 1.5 MILLION B.C.

Bearded and hairy, Neanderthal Man was the first long-distance runner, hunting antelope and other wild animals in Africa on foot. The chase lasted many hours and miles until the exhausted animal could no longer go on. Neanderthal Man ran barefoot, clad only in a loincloth made of animal hides.

GREEK MILITARY COURIER, 400 B.C.

The Greek Military Courier likely ran in full battle armor, although he surely shed the dead weight as the miles rolled on. He carried vital messages between commanders in the field, and between the battlefront and Athens or Sparta. Duty required him to run tremendous distances over the course of a day and night. While he may have worn sandals in camp, he too ran barefoot.

APACHE BRAVE, 1870S

Another barefoot runner, Apache Brave of the American Southwest started running as a boy and never really stopped. When he was young, he competed in footraces as part of tribal ceremonies. Growing older, he used his speed to track and hunt animals across the desert, deliver messages, and chase down or run away from enemy tribes or the US Cavalry. He also was a gifted horseman.

MODERN RUNNING GUY, CIRCA NOW

Bearded and with clumps of back hair similar to Neanderthal Man, Modern Running Guy also runs for his food, although it may just be down to the local Starbucks for a latte and a gluten-free marshmallow bar. He is easy to spot jogging around the reservoir, because he is totally on trend in the way he looks and the gear he uses:

- Sunglasses (to ease glare so his muscles don't tense up)
- Titanium necklace (to increase blood flow)

- Nasal breathing strip
- Fitbit
- Smartphone (for calling people to tell them he's running)
- Ear buds
- Tech shirt (never wears just plain cotton anymore)
- Knee-high compression socks (also for improved blood flow)
- Gloves (to make sure his fingers don't miss out on that good blood flow)
- Orthotics
- And, of course, a pair of $195 neon-orange Nike Frees to make him *feel* like he's running barefoot.

WHAT'S WRONG WITH RUNNERS?

JUST ASK THESE PEOPLE. THEY'LL TELL YOU.

Runners, like attendees at a TED conference, are very much into self-improvement. They hope to get into better shape, look and feel better, and meet some people and have some fun while they're at it.

You wouldn't think such modest and admirable goals would cause such a stink, and yet they do. Some outspoken *opinionistas* feel com-

pelled to dump large buckets of snark at the feet of runners, whom they accuse of assorted transgressions such as:

THEY POST TOO MUCH ON SOCIAL MEDIA.

And what they post is too often of a self-serving nature. This is a pet peeve of Chicago blogger Dan Tello, who doesn't object to people exercising; he just doesn't want to hear about it. "Go for it," he advises. "Just don't tell me about it with an aura of smugness like you just graduated Med School." The *Spectator's* Julie Bindel likens chronic posting to "a self-congratulatory wank-fest," while sarcasm drips like beads of sweat from the pen of the *New Yorker's* Jaclyn Loraso.

"If a runner collapses in joy at the finish line but no one Instagrams it, did she collapse at all?" she writes. "Post photos plus commentary on your morning run, your evening run, your vacation run; show us your bibs, your medals, your post-run beer. Let us see your sneakered feet—on grass, on sand, in the snow, on a track. Share it all! Everyone you know is incredibly invested in your new endeavor."

THEY SHOW OFF BY WEARING THEIR RACING MEDALS.

Runners win medals when they finish or place high in a race, a source of justifiable pride for them. But not to blogger Lauren Passell, a runner herself. "I actually have a theory," she confides, "that how long you wear your running medal after a race is in direct correlation to how big of a douchebag you are."

THEY ENGAGE IN SHOWY DISPLAYS OF WEALTH AND CONSUMERISM.

"I detest the fancy, expensive water bottles they carry in one hand," remarks Bindel, "their iPad in the other." (No mean feat, that.) Chad Stafko of the *Wall Street Journal* disses runners for wearing track suits and other athletic clothing emblazoned with logos. "This apparel serves a clear purpose," he huffs. "We can look at them and immediately know that the person wearing it is a runner."

THE SHORTS THAT MEN WEAR ARE TOO SHORT.

After apparently close observation of her subjects, Bindel says she dislikes tight Lycra running shorts on men because "you can see their religion." The *Washington Post*'s Matthew Rennie agrees. He cannot abide men who "prance around in shorts that show more thigh than Lady Gaga's meat dress. But the headbands are definitely a nice look," he adds with a dig.

THEY PUT "26.2" OR "13.1" BUMPER STICKERS ON THEIR CARS.

These are, in Dan Tello's words, "smug bumper stickers for smug people. Seriously, have you ever seen one of the '26.2' bumper stickers on a car that was not a Prius or a Subaru?" Stafko swings the club harder: "There is only one reason running aficionados display the stickers. They want the rest of us to know about their long-distance feats. So let me be the first to offer my hearty congratulations. I'd even offer to give them a pat on the back—once they're done doing it themselves."

THEY ARE, ON THE WHOLE, ANNOYING, FOOLISH, AND IDIOTIC.

Bindel: "They annoy dogs, drivers, cyclists, and get in the way of wheelchairs and groups of people out for a stroll enjoying the weather." Stafko: "Why would someone want to get up at 5 a.m. and run 10 miles adorned with fluorescent tape to avoid being struck by someone who has the good sense to use a car for a 10 mile journey?" Loraso: "When people see your progress from utter sloth to still-slightly-paunchy gazelle, you'll inspire a whole new crop of runners. They'll think, 'If that idiot can do it, I can probably do it.' You could be that idiot!"

Last word goes to the manic creator of *Young Frankenstein* and *Blazing Saddles*, Mel Brooks, who has no beef with runners per se. He simply sees no reason to do what they do. At all. Ever. At any time.

"Never run for a bus," he explains. "There will always be another."

HOW TO STOP A DOG

Dogs are members of the family, warm and devoted companions always eager for a run. Their need to exercise encourages you to get up and out and take them with you when you go. They serve as protection too, especially for solo females traveling in unfamiliar neighborhoods.

On the other hand . . .

When they do not belong to you or they're unleashed, dogs can be pests or worse. They come out of nowhere, lunge at you unexpectedly, snap, growl, bark, and despite their owner's protestations, they can bite. "Every dog that has bitten me was a dog that didn't bite," says Pete Magill, an accomplished age-group runner. "Their owners told me so—often as the blood dripped down my leg from Fido's fang marks."

Bill Rodgers always carried a heavy set of keys when he ran to ward off any unwelcome canine advances. One day he was in a workout with Alberto Salazar around Boston. This was in the days when Rodgers was king of the marathon world and Salazar was a young aspirant to the throne, and both ran for the GBTC—Greater Boston Track Club.

Suddenly a "huge Great Dane, a dog from hell," in Salazar's words, came roaring straight at Salazar who stopped and froze. The dog appeared ready to lunge at him when Rodgers hurled his keys at him and scared him away. To this day Salazar credits Rodgers with saving him from severe harm.

THE BACKBONE OF THE COMMUNITY

7 REASONS WHY YOU SHOULD CONSIDER JOINING A RUNNING CLUB

Running clubs are the backbone of the running community. They organize races and stock them with volunteers. They hold weekly meet-ups for informal runs, sponsor coaching programs, go on trips, support elite teams, and function as a social network for runners and their families.

They get together and drink and eat, too.

Even so, some runners, being natural loners and non-joiners—and dare we say it, perhaps a bit snobbish?—prefer to keep their distance. Consider these seven reasons for joining a running club:

1. YOU MEET PEOPLE.

This is what happened to writer and marathoner Rachel Toor. "I've never been much of a joiner, but when I found something I loved doing—and realized there were other people who shared my enthusiasm—I joined a running club. By becoming a runner, I was welcomed by strangers as a comrade."

2. YOU MEET DIFFERENT KINDS OF PEOPLE.

Community running clubs are, as the name implies, open to the community. Lots of different people—people you might not ordinarily get a chance to meet—belong. Young elites too. Most clubs have special programs for the young, the gifted, and the fast.

3. THEY SPEAK YOUR LANGUAGE.

These new comrades—these new brothers and sisters in arms you are meeting—they all speak your language. Again, the perspicacious Ms. Toor: "Running gave me a *lingua franca*, a common language to share with new acquaintances."

4. THEY SHARE YOUR GOALS.

"The most important factor for motivation is goal setting," says Francie Larrieu Smith. "You should always have a goal." Smith's goals as a distance runner included making the US Olympic team, which she did five times. But she is the first to admit that she didn't do it on her own; she had lots of help along the way, and that's where a club can prove useful. Whether your goals are Larrieu Smith–like or of a less-ambitious nature, you can connect with people with similar goals.

SNOB ASIDE

Larrieu Smith's career parallels the growth and development of women's running. At the 1972 Munich Games, when she was nineteen, she competed in the 1,500 meters, then the longest Olympic distance for women. By the 1992 Barcelona Games, her fifth and final Olympics, the women's marathon had become an established event and she finished twelfth in the race. She now coaches both the men's and women's track and cross-country teams at Southwestern University in Texas.

5. YOU CAN MAKE VALUABLE CONNECTIONS AT A CLUB.

Generally speaking, the people who run, the people who belong to running clubs, are a motivated group. The settings on their internal Bunsen burners are turned up pretty high. They include techie entrepreneurs, savvy business pros, nonprofit CEOs, community leaders, tradespeople, cops, teachers, writers, artists, students, retirees with remarkable life stories. You can make a connection in a running club that can help you outside of it.

6. IT'S A FAMILY ATMOSPHERE.

You attend parties and potlucks, go on trips, and socialize aplenty at pubs and other gathering places. There are events, author talks, other activities. Nor is everyone a runner; the nonrunning spouses and family members often participate too, contributing to a family atmosphere, especially at smaller clubs.

7. YOU CAN DO FOR OTHERS.

Some of what you do at a club may not strictly be about your running, as critically important as that is at all times. Club-sponsored races and events raise money for the club as well as worthy causes. Thus, volunteering for a race can help your club and community. Like all nonprofits, running clubs suffer from a chronic shortage of talented individuals who are willing to serve on the board of directors, go to meetings, guide policy. If you're really feeling in a generous mood, you can volunteer for that too.

2135
MARATHON

THE SNOB 21

A TASTING FLIGHT OF RUNNING CLUBS ACROSS THE UNITED STATES

A tasting flight of wine or beer is a selection of small tastes that allows people to sample a variety of what the winery or craft brewpub is making and pouring for its guests.

Consider this a tasting flight of running clubs across the United States. With close to two thousand clubs to choose from, here are brief looks at twenty-one of the best.

ALARC

ALARC's founder is a man named Bill Wenmark, one of those extraordinary, larger-than-life figures who seem to populate the world of running. A physician, decorated Marine combat corpsman, healthcare industry leader, entrepreneur, runner, and marathon coach, he founded this Minneapolis club when he was president of the American Lung Association. It promotes fitness and cardiovascular health and teaches marathon training. Alarc.com

ATLANTA TRACK CLUB

The Atlanta Track Club is the power of the South, second only to New York Road Runners in membership with twenty-four thousand members. It sponsors thirty races a year, the biggest of which is the Peachtree Road Race, the biggest 10K in the world. Every Fourth of July sixty thousand runners and walkers take over downtown Atlanta. AtlantaTrackClub.org

AUSTIN RUNNERS CLUB

Austin's unofficial motto is "Keep Austin Weird." The ARC maintains a youthful rock vibe consistent with the city's counterculture traditions. It doesn't take itself too seriously, which is an admirable quality for both people and running clubs, holding what it calls "ship of fools" runs on Town Lake Trail. The runs begin at five in the morning, and because Austin is one of the best running cities in the country, you will have lots of company should you decide to join in. AustinRunners.org

B.A.A.

These three initials are synonymous with the history of the marathon in this country. They stand for the Boston Athletic Association, the organization that has run the world's oldest annual marathon since its inception in 1897. Need we say more? Baa.org

BOULDER ROAD RUNNERS

Boulder is a lot like Austin, only with big, snowy Rocky Mountain peaks in the neighborhood. It's a college town that attracts elite runners who enjoy its casual atmosphere and the opportunity to crank up their VO2 max at 5,400 feet above sea level. The Boulder Road Runners is smack dab in the middle of the scene. BoulderRoadRunners.org

CARA

Writer Liz Plosser calls CARA—Chicago Area Runners Association—"the big momma" of Chicago running. It's fair to call it the Big Daddy too. Beginning as a small club in the late 1970s, it has grown into a nine-thousand-member mother ship for all things running in Chicagoland. CaraRuns.org

CLUB NORTHWEST, SEATTLE RUNNING CLUB

Club Northwest, in Seattle, is one of the oldest running clubs in the Pacific Northwest, which is saying something in a region with Eugene, Portland, and Spokane. ClubNorthwest.org

Across town, the Seattle Running Club focuses more on the trails than the roads. After a day of slogging in the hills, its members head over to Flying Lion Brewing in Columbia City for discounted pints of beer and ale, one of many glorious tie-ins between running clubs and drinking establishments across the globe. SeattleRunningClub.org

DSE RUNNERS, PAMAKIDS

The founder and inspirational beacon of DSE—San Francisco's oldest running club—was another of those grand old men of running, Walt Stack, a colorful and beloved octogenarian marathoner whose slogan—"Start slow, and taper off"—remains the motto of back-of-the-packers everywhere. DseRunners.com

Another San Francisco club with a long tradition is the family-oriented Pamakids, whose name derives from "Pa"—fathers—"Ma"—mothers—and kids. Pamakids.org

FLORIDA TRACK CLUB

When you're talking glamorous T-shirts to wear during America's first running boom of the 1970s, few could match the glory of the white Florida Track Club singlet with the big orange in the center. Frank Shorter and long and lanky Jack Bacheler ran first and ninth respectively in the 1972 Olympic marathon in Munich, and they both wore Florida's colors when they weren't wearing America's. Based in Gainesville, FTC has more of a community-oriented approach today, but its members still proudly sport around with that big orange on their chests. FloridaTrackClub.org

QUOTABLE SNOB

"There's always the feeling of getting stronger. I think that's what keeps me going."

—FRANK SHORTER, during his glory days

GBTC

Around the same time that Florida's oranges were popping up at the front of road races, so were GBTC tees. If you showed up in a GBTC T-shirt—you know, the one with the winged shoe on the front with "Greater Boston" above it and "Track Club" below, or maybe just a big "BOSTON" across the front with "GBTC" underneath—everybody else in the race figured you were fast. And you probably were. Bill Rodgers wore one for a time. So did Alberto Salazar. Three of the top five guys at Boston 1978 wore one; so did four of the top ten the next

year. Those glory days are gone, but the club continues to shine as one of New England's best. Gbtc.org

GREATER LONG ISLAND RUNNING CLUB

Live in Nassau or Suffolk Counties? If you do, you probably already know that the go-to guide for racing and running there is *Long Island Footnotes*, published by the GLRC. Its thirty-five hundred members make it the biggest club on Long Island. Glirc.org

L.A. LEGGERS

While reporting on the 1989 Los Angeles Marathon, radio broadcaster Bob Scott, who was also running the race, noticed that an alarming number of the participants were badly out of shape and had no clue what they were doing. This inspired him to start the Leggers, which is based in Santa Monica but draws runners of all abilities from all around Southern California. LaLeggers.org

LIBERTY ATHLETIC CLUB

Another proud and historic New England tradition: The first and oldest running club for women in the United States, founded in 1948. Today Liberty AC members work out at the indoor and outdoor tracks at Harvard U. Those members, incidentally, represent a Hall of Fame of New England and American women's running, including 1992 Olympic Games 10,000 meter bronze medalist Lynn Jennings and 1984 Olympic marathon gold medalist Joan Benoit Samuelson. LibertyAC.org

MONTGOMERY COUNTY ROAD RUNNERS CLUB

Deep in the heart of suburban Rockville, Maryland, the MCRRC boasts a healthy membership count of five thousand, drawing runners from all around the Baltimore—Washington D.C. metro areas. The club's

oval-shaped logo depicts a road curling off into the distance. "The meatball" is what everyone calls it. Mcrrc.org

NYRR

When NYRR was founded in 1958, it was a club—the New York Road Runners Club. A club it is no more, at least in name, for it has removed the word from its identity, which is probably apt. As others have pointed out, NYRR is less of a club and more of a nonprofit corporation with forty-five thousand–plus members, scores of runs and races, and an annual budget in the tens of millions. But is its signature event better than Boston? Or Chicago? See our tale of the tape, "New York v. Boston," on pages 140–42 and decide. Nyrr.org

OREGON ROAD RUNNERS CLUB

Like so many running clubs, the ORRC started in connection with a marathon, in its case the Trail's End in Oregon. A group of enthusiasts helped put on (and run in) the first-ever Trail's End in 1978, and in the process they organized themselves into a club that has grown to one thousand runners, the largest in the West. Home is Beaverton, site of Nike corporate headquarters. Orrc.net

OREGON TRACK CLUB

OTC is another of those clubs, like B.A.A. or NYRR, identifiable by their initials alone. And like those two clubs, OTC represents excellence in the sport. Founded by Bill Bowerman, the OTC helped make Eugene the distance-running capital of the West, aka Track Town USA. Among its activities are maintaining Pre's Trail, the Eugene running trail that honors the memory of Steve Prefontaine. Oregon TrackClub.runnerspace.com

ROAD RUNNERS CLUB OF AMERICA

Not a running club per se, the RRCA is the oldest (since 1958) and biggest national association of running clubs. Based in Arlington, Virginia, it represents more than one thousand member clubs and two hundred thousand runners, sponsors a multitude of events every year, and is a good contact if you're looking for a club or race in your area. Rrca.org

YOUNG INVOLVED PHILADELPHIA

In 2000 a group of recent college graduates in Philly formed YIP to influence the city's future direction and policies. It has won wide praise since then for its civic leadership and now has six thousand members, many of whom are runners. They meet weekly for runs and afterward get together for drinks and power networking. YoungInvolvedPhila.org

FAMILY FEUD

JOGGERS V. REAL RUNNERS

Real Runners and Joggers are the Montagues and Capulets of the sport, forever quarreling and sniping. Real Runners regard Joggers as dilettantes who lower the standards of their calling, while Joggers wish Real Runners would lighten up and not take themselves so seriously.

A plague on both their houses? No, we say! In the interests of healing this rift and promoting togetherness, we present this thumbnail guide to show how each side looks at various aspects of the running world. Can't we all just get along?

SUBJECT	REAL RUNNERS	JOGGERS
Favorite race	Marathon	5K
Walk part of long race?	Never!	Why not?
Training schedule	Every day	Weekends (maybe)
What they'll be doing at 5 a.m. tomorrow	Working out	Sleeping it off
Favorite running movie	*Without Limits*	*McFarland USA*
View of pain	Transcend it	Buckle under it
Race goal	Win, crush rivals	Finish
Running a hill late in a marathon	Dies slowly	Dies quickly
Favorite post-race activity	Drinking beer	Sucking air
Running style	Light & efficient, like the Kenyans	Whatever
Animal they most resemble when running	Gazelle	Budweiser Clydesdale
Run barefoot?	Has done it	"You crazy? I spent 200 bucks on these shoes!"
Body part that hurts the most	Knees	All of them
Favorite running book	*Running Snob*	*Running Snob*

DATING A RUNNER

THE DO'S AND DON'TS
OF LOVE ON THE ROADS

Alan and Shayne Culpepper. Kara and Adam Goucher. Deena and Andrew Kastor. Paula Radcliffe and Gary Lough. Sileshi Sihine and Tirunesh Dibaba. Allan and Julia Webb.

These famous distance-running couples, elite runners, and coaches all, have shown they can mix running with romance and make it work. But it is not easy, as every couple will testify. Here are a few do's and don'ts of dating and romance that will help you get through the rough spots.

DO: DATE A RUNNER.

This is not strictly necessary in order to have a successful love life, but it does offer clear advantages. As blogger Sally Tamarkin notes, all runners believe that "any problem can be solved with a run." Thus when the two of you encounter relationship issues you can face them head-on by going out for a run together. By the time you get back, your problems may be magically solved. Your shared belief in the power of running daily extends even to the climate. "You look forward to bad weather so you can say you ran through it," says Tamarkin.

DON'T: ASK THEM TO CONVERT.

If the person you are seeing does *not* run, do not try to talk him or her into it, at least not in the early stages of the relationship. Columnist Beth Risdon urges all nonrunners to actively resist the pleas of their running partner: "If you date a runner," she says, "he/she will inevitably try to turn you into a runner. This is a personal mission because they want you to love running as much as they do. Stay strong." One reason for her coolness toward men who run is the snot rockets they frequently blow from their nose.

QUOTABLE SNOB

"Runners often do crazy things like use the word *fartlek*, piss on the side of roads, and lather themselves with Vaseline."

—WRITER LAUREN PASSELL,
offering another reason to avoid male runners

DON'T: TALK TOO MUCH ABOUT RUNNING ON A FIRST DATE.

Fitness gurus Alexandra ONeale and Michelle Toglia go on and on about the virtues of runners as dating material for women. "Have you seen a runner's body?" they wrote in an online column. "Baby got track. Bonus: They're constantly sweating, shirtless and wearing short shorts." They also raved about the "natural glow" of runners, the good causes they support, how self-confident they are, even how many brain cells they have. All these things are true, but it's still good to ask a question or two about your date to show you're interested in her too.

DO: GO ON RUNNING DATES.

Running dates are a terrific way to get to know someone, rather than the usual go out for drinks or coffee routine. That was how Martin Dugard, a runner, author, and high school track coach, came to meet and fall in love with his future wife Callie. He admits, however, to two critical mistakes in this regard. One was constantly miscounting the number of miles they were running, "thinking that 2 miles were 1 and 4 miles were 2 or 3." Since he was the one keeping track of the mileage for the pair, Callie thought he was clueless. His other big mistake was believing that Callie would naturally enjoy his running methods. Whereas he loves to meander, not hewing to the same route every time, she does not. For her "a route is a route is a route." And when he led her all over the map, it frustrated her.

DO: SAY SWEET THINGS TO HER.

Despite his mistakes, it turned out all right for Dugard, who remembered to say sweet things to Callie, and this never hurts. "Like all the best things in life," he says with the words of a poet, "a great run becomes even more wondrous with someone you love."

DON'T: FOR WOMEN, DO NOT—REPEAT: DO NOT—GO TO BED RIGHT AWAY WITH EVERY MALE RUNNER YOU MEET, EVEN IF HE LOOKS LIKE CHANNING TATUM AND POETIZES LIKE CYRANO.

To refer, again, to the research of ONeale-Toglia, they say that because male runners possess high levels of cardiovascular health, this makes them champions in bed. They are, and we quote, "sex gods." But again, ladies, you'll hate yourself in the morning if you give in instantly to temptation. Make that sex god wait. If he has to suffer, so be it. He's a runner. He's used to it.

DON'T: GIVE HIM FOOT RUBS.

Along these same lines, do not give in to his pathetic requests for foot rubs, for we all know where such acts of intimacy lead. Besides, "runners have disgusting feet," as Beth Risdon observes. "A runner's feet will likely be covered in blisters and bunions."

DO: THINK OF RUNNING WHEN YOU SAY "I DO."

Susan and Phil, a Canadian couple who met through an online dating service, exchanged vows during a half marathon in Ontario, Canada. They and twenty members of the wedding party who were running with them stopped at the halfway point and conducted the ceremony. The groom wore a technical tuxedo T-shirt and the bride looked heavenly in a Wonder Girl tank top, Capri skirt, and long-sleeve shirt. The guests all wore purple tees that said "Going the Distance." They went on to finish the race and hold a big party and reception.

DO: HAVE CHILDREN, LOTS AND LOTS OF THEM.

That is, of course, when the time is right and you and your mate are truly in love. For you will find that children will be a boon to your running career. Proof of this is George Sheehan, the great running philosopher and *Runner's World* columnist who had twelve kids. *Twelve kids!* Can there be any doubt that runners are indeed sex gods? That is also surely why Dr. Sheehan took so often to the roads: to get the hell out of the house and away from all those kids.

HOW TO RAISE A RUNNER IN 10 EASY STEPS

Running is, at heart, a child's activity, and infants and small children are everywhere to be found at a race or festival—begging for a hot chocolate or to get their face painted, pouting if they don't get their way, demanding release from the confines of a stroller, crying, throwing tantrums, acting up, spreading germs.

It's a beautiful thing.

Despite the challenges, children are one of the true blessings of life (as George Sheehan might have told his wife as he was leaving to go on one of his long, long runs). As a matched set with our dating advice column, here are ten easy steps to turning that little darling you've got attached to a leash into a runner like you:

1. Read the children's story "The Tortoise and the Hare" over and over to her, emphasizing the strategic racing brilliance of the tortoise.
2. Take family road trips to Hayward Field in Eugene, Heartbreak Hill in Boston, and other sites of historic running significance.
3. Get baby booties with Vibram soles.
4. Discuss training methods and the importance of keeping a meticulous training log while changing, feeding, and burping her.
5. The saying on her baby bib should be aspirational in nature. One suggestion: "New York City 2040," the year she becomes fully grown and can run the marathon.
6. Talk in kilometers, not miles—5K, 10K, 15K. A marathon is 42.195K.
7. Advise her not to spit out her SpaghettiOs or smear them all over her face because she needs them for "carbo-loading." Also, while toasting Eggo Waffles in the morning, inspire her with the instructional tale of Bill Bowerman and the invention of the waffle running shoe, encouraging her entrepreneurial instincts.
8. Teach geography at a young age, pointing out how all the great cities of Europe and the world—London, Paris, Berlin, Tokyo, etc.—have marathons and half marathons.
9. Paper her bedroom walls with posters of role models such as Shalane Flanagan, Desiree Linden, and Meb Keflezighi, noting how they are not only good runners, they're good human beings too.
10. Push her in a stroller when you run. After you're done, take a moment to speak to her quietly and sincerely about how all of this—the jogging path, the fresh air, the low pulse rate, the high VO2 max—will be hers someday.

THE SNOB 12

A DOZEN RUNNING RACES AND TEAMS THAT HELP RAISE MILLIONS FOR CHARITY

From 5K fun runs to 100-mile ultras, virtually every race raises money for charities and nonprofit organizations. Charities and nonprofits of every description partner with races to raise money for their organizations and the good work they do.

Runners can be justifiably proud of their good works as well. Through their entry fees, their contributions, their fundraising, and in many other ways, they raise hundreds of millions of dollars *every year* for programs that aid military veterans, fight cancer, improve education for children, provide shelter for the homeless, support the victims of terrorism, assist shut-in seniors, help the environment, and more. The twelve races listed here represent only a tiny cross-section of the vast contributions of the running community at large.

THE LEMON RUN

Before her first birthday Alexandra "Alex" Scott was diagnosed with neuroblastoma, a type of childhood cancer. By her fourth birthday, still battling the disease, she and her brother decided to set up a lemonade stand on the sidewalk outside their house in the town of Bala Cynwyd, Pennsylvania. Their goal was to raise money to help children

suffering from cancer and for cancer research. Word got around, and people in town contributed two thousand dollars to their cause.

Alex's story—how she was trying to help other kids fight a disease that she herself had—stirred people around the country and world. Other kids set up lemonade stands and sent her the money they earned; individuals and companies added their support. By 2004 the Alex Lemonade Stand Foundation had raised more than one million dollars.

The Lemon Run in Fairmount Park in Philadelphia benefits the cancer-fighting research of the foundation. Two years ago it attracted 3,250 participants and raised $370,000. Alex died at age eight. Alexs Lemonade.org

TEAM IN TRAINING

Georgia Cleland was another little girl hit hard by disease; she developed leukemia at age two. Fortunately it later went into remission, and she went on to lead a healthy life. But there's more to the story.

After Georgia came through the worst part of her struggle, her father Bruce Cleland wanted to do something to help the Leukemia & Lymphoma Society (LLS), which had provided support for his daughter and their family during her illness. What he decided to do was form a team of runners to participate in the 1988 New York City Marathon. Everyone on the team would raise money for the LLS, soliciting from family members, friends, fellow employees, and others.

Cleland's idea surpassed his own and everyone else's expectations. He and his team of thirty-eight runners raised $322,000 for the LLS that year, and it became the basis for Team in Training, an ongoing sports training program that raises money for the organization. Members receive coaching and other benefits as they train for endurance events around the country. To date more than 600,000 people—runners, cyclists, triathletes, hikers—have raised $875 million for blood cancer research and to support families like the Clelands. Other nonprofits have also adopted similar team training techniques to raise money for their causes. TeaminTraining.org

RUNNING 4 BABIES

Parents who have ever had a baby go into an NICU—neonatal intensive care unit—know how scary that can be. Babies are not admitted to an NICU unless their condition is serious or needs urgent attention. This 5K trail run and walk in Traverse City, Michigan, pays tribute to the everyday heroes of NICUs—doctors, nurses, staff—and financially supports the neonatal intensive care unit at Munson Medical Center in town. In gestures of honoring and remembrance, some runners put the names of children on the back of their T-shirts—the names of babies who were born prematurely and survived, and the little ones who did not. Running4Babies.com

CELLMATES ON THE RUN

Cellmates refers not to prisoners in jail as one might think, but rather to scientific research into the nature of insulin-producing cells and finding a cure for type 1 diabetes. Founded by Jose Oberholzer, chief of cell transplant surgery at the Chicago College of Medicine at the University of Illinois, Cellmates on the Run is the running team of the Chicago Diabetes Project, whose members have raised hun-

dreds of thousands of dollars with the motto: "Outrun diabetes."
ChicagoDiabetesProject.org

RACE FOR THE CURE

From death comes life. The end is not the end of everything; sometimes it's a beginning too. So it was with Nancy Brinker as she watched her sister Susan, once vibrant and full of life, put up a fight against breast cancer and lose. Taking arms against the disease and vowing to honor her sister's memory, in 1980 Nancy formed the Susan G. Komen Foundation, which has become the largest breast cancer organization in the world, funding research, education, and support programs in the United States and other countries. Its Race for the Cure series has played a monumental role in this effort. Beginning in Dallas with two hundred runners and walkers, there are now 150 annual Race for the Cure events with one million–plus participants. The series has raised more than 2.6 billion dollars. Komen.org

SEMPER FI 5K

In the early years of the Iraq and Afghanistan Wars, Karen Guenther, a registered nurse and the wife of an active-duty Marine who was serving overseas, was stationed at Camp Pendleton, a Marine Corps base north of San Diego. In her duties she treated a number of seriously wounded Marines and other servicepeople, steadily coming to realize that these young men and women were going to need help—and lots of it. Not just medical treatment, although that was vital, but also psychological, financial, and practical support as they reentered American society as civilians.

Together with other Camp Pendleton nurses and military spouses, she formed the Semper Fi Fund, a national organization that provides financial and other assistance to wounded vets of all branches of the US Armed Forces and their families. Fittingly this 5K, which raises money for the fund, starts near the Lincoln Memorial in Washington D.C. and takes place on Armed Forces Day. SemperFiFund.org

RUN TO REMEMBER

Also not to be forgotten: the police officers, firefighters, and others who have paid the ultimate sacrifice in the line of duty. This 5K run and walk along the Chicago waterfront honors the memories of Chicago's finest who were killed while doing their job and supports their families and survivors. The beneficiary is the Chicago Police Memorial Foundation, whose motto is "Never Forget." Two years ago it raised $175,000. Many other similarly named "Run to Remember" races are held around the country to support police, firefighter, and veteran causes. CPDMemorial.org

GIRLS ON THE RUN

Founded by Molly Barker in 1996 in Charlotte, this international organization supports fitness education for girls. It consists of 120,000 volunteers coaching and mentoring 178,000 girls around the United States and other countries. Girls graduate from the after school program by walking and/or running 5Ks. In addition to volunteering their time and expertise as coaches, runners have raised close to one million dollars for the organization in races. GirlsOnTheRun.org

TEAM WORLD VISION

Team World Vision is an international Christian humanitarian organization that began in 1950. Originally its goal was to provide food and shelter for orphaned children in Africa and elsewhere. Over the years its mission has evolved into community development, particularly digging and building water wells in places of extreme poverty in Africa where there is no clean water to drink. Unsanitary water is a leading cause of disease and death in those areas. The first World

Vision team appeared at the Chicago Marathon, and others are running in races all over the map. TeamWorldVision.org

JINGLE BELL RUN

London Marathon race director Dave Bedford has said that running in charity races makes runners seem "less nerdy" to the general public. No one would ever accuse someone who ties jingle bells to his shoes, dresses up as Santa Claus, or dons reindeer antlers as being nerdy, not when he's doing so much good and having so much fun in this national series of 5K fun runs that has raised close to eight million dollars for the Arthritis Foundation. Arthritis.org

QUOTABLE SNOB

"I have two doctors: my left leg and my right."

—SIR GEORGE M. TREVELYAN, an esteemed British historian who was a competitive cross-country runner in his youth

BACK ON MY FEET

Anne Mahlum was a runner, in her mid-twenties, living and working in Philadelphia. As she ran around the streets on her daily workouts she noticed, as every city dweller does, the homeless people camped out on sidewalks or in the alcoves of buildings or in parks. But instead of ignoring them she wondered if there was a way to help them.

Running improves my life, she thought. Could it help improve their lives too?

This intriguing question led to the formation, in 2007, of Back on My Feet, a national organization designed to help the homeless through

running. Here is how it works: Back on My Feet assists homeless people in getting jobs, housing, and becoming self-sufficient. But to become eligible for its programs, they must live in a shelter or mission for at least a month, at which time they sign a contract with the following stipulations. They must show up at six in the morning three days a week, be on time, respect themselves and others, and—here's the bottom line—go on a run or jog on these days. Their running becomes the catalyst for making other positive changes in their life.

Back On My Feet gets help from nonhomeless runners in two critical ways. One, they enter races as teams and individuals and raise money for the group. Two, they volunteer to run with the homeless on their early morning workouts to encourage, support, and mentor them. BackOnMyFeet.org

DIRTY DOG TRAIL RUN

Along with the violence and the threat of violence they must endure, domestic violence victims can sometimes suffer another blow—the loss of their pets. When a domestic violence victim must flee the house for his or her safety, finding refuge in an emergency shelter or home, their dog or cat may have nowhere to go. The Dirty Dog Trail Run of Midland City, Michigan, supports a local animal shelter as well as victims of domestic violence who have pets. The shelter takes in the pets, mostly dogs, during a crisis, thanks in part to the race fees paid by runners. Dogs, clean or dirty, can join this Upper Peninsula run as long as they're on a leash. DirtyDogTrailRun.ItsYourRace.com

RUNNING SNOB QUIZ #1: JOAN BENOIT SAMUELSON

Joan Benoit Samuelson is a wife, mother, author, motivational speaker, consultant, and one of the best marathoners of all time. "Running," she says, "has provided me with countless challenges and rewards, as have my marriage and the birth of my children." Our first quiz touches on the two major currents of her life— running and family. Answers follow the quiz.

1. Close friends of the 5-foot-3, 105-pound Benoit Samuelson call her by a nickname, the same name as a character in a 1980s sitcom. What is it?
   a. Laverne
   b. Shirley
   c. Fonzie
   d. Joanie
2. Benoit Samuelson cites several women as being role models in her running career. Which of these women was a role model for her? More than one answer permitted.
   a. Grete Waitz
   b. Mary Decker Slaney
   c. Francie Larrieu Smith
   d. Christine Clark

3. Most runners of her generation remember how she won the gold medal in the Women's Marathon in the 1984 Los Angeles Olympic Games, the first women's Olympic marathon ever. But the second-place finisher in that race was also a female running pioneer. Can you name her?

   a. Kathrine Switzer

   b. Grete Waitz

   c. Nina Kuscik

   d. Mary Decker Slaney

4. Joan suffered a number of injuries in her career and has the surgical scars to prove it. What body part has she NOT had surgery on?

   a. knee

   b. left Achilles tendon

   c. right Achilles tendon

   d. hip

5. At her peak, Joan covered 110 miles a week, running twice a day, morning and evening. She would run a 10-miler in the morning followed by a track workout in the afternoon. Given this regimen, did she make the following statements about training? Yes or no.

   a. "It is important to fully understand the difference between training and fatigue. Do not work into the pain zone."

   b. "Keep varying the program. Your body will tell you what to do."

6. "Among my women running friends," wrote Joan when she was younger, "we talk about the M word." The M word meant two things. One was Marathon. What did the other M word stand for?

   a. Men

   b. Marriage

   c. Menstruation

   d. Meals

7. "I'll never forget one special day," she recalled once. "I felt I could have run forever." That night she gave birth to her daughter. How far did she run that day?

   a. 2 miles

   b. 5 miles

   c. 10 miles

   d. 13.1 miles, a half marathon

8. Here are four statements about running and pregnancy. Joan said three of them; the other was made by Dr. Joan Ullyot, herself a famous running pioneer, author, and medical doctor. Name the quote by Ullyot.

   a. "Gazelles run when they're pregnant. Why should it be any different for women?"

   b. "You have everything to gain and nothing to lose by taking a low-key approach to training during and after pregnancy."

   c. "I often felt better running while pregnant than when I wasn't pregnant. Everything seemed to mesh together for me."

   d. "I wasn't running only for myself but with someone else in mind."

9. This runner-turned-athlete is one of America's all-time best middle-distance runners, a former Olympian, and one-time high school running sensation. What's more, he and his wife named their daughter after Joan, a tribute to the example she set for runners. Who is he?.

   a. Alan Webb

   b. Meb Keflezighi

   c. Dathan Ritzenhein

   d. Dave Scott

10. A strong believer in lifelong fitness, Joan achieved a notable personal goal after turning fifty years old. What was it?

   a. She finished a triathlon.

   b. She threw out the opening pitch at Fenway Park, home of her beloved Boston Red Sox.

   c. She ran a marathon with her children.

   d. She ran a marathon in under 2:50.

ANSWERS: 1. d; 2 a, b, c; 3. b; 4. d; 5. Yes; 6. c; 7. b; 8. a; 9. a; 10. d

CHAPTER TWO

Running and You

There is more to running than just running. There is an emotional, psychological, and even spiritual side to it. Many runners would say it is less a physical act and more a mental one. It requires motivation to do daily, and to get and stay inspired runners must dig deep into themselves, their goals, and their aspirations. This chapter explores the journey of self-discovery and self-expression every person embarks on when he or she becomes a runner.

A MOST CEREBRAL FORM OF EXERCISE

7 NONPHYSICAL BENEFITS OF RUNNING

The esteemed marathoner and writer Amby Burfoot has written that running is "a mental activity, not a physical activity," which may strike nonrunners as a rather peculiar thing to say. How can such a physical act be nonphysical?

Most people who run regularly, though, will see the sense of the statement, in part because they receive so many nonphysical benefits from running. Here are seven ways that running provides its practitioners a mental and emotional lift.

1. IT HELPS YOU THINK.

It clarifies and sharpens your thoughts. In 1959, British novelist Alan Sillitoe wrote "The Loneliness of the Long Distance Runner," the story from which the famous phrase derives. It was also made into a movie, for which the clear-thinking Sillitoe wrote the script. It's about a rebellious working-class Brit who gets in trouble with the law but finds some peace in his life through running. "The long distance run-

ning lark is the best of all," wrote Sillitoe in the vernacular. "Because it makes me think so good."

2. IT STIRS CREATIVITY.

Like so many others, Oz Pearlman uses running to get the creative juices flowing in his job. His job is a little different from most though; he's a magician and mentalist. "A lot of my bursts of creativity happen when I run," he says. "A run is where I love to try everything out. I pantomime and talk to myself, trying to coax out what I'll do in my act." The Wizard of Oz almost but not quite won *America's Got Talent* one season (he took third), but he has finished both the Leadville 100 and Western States 100, which are far more impressive feats anyway.

3. IT BOOSTS SELF-ESTEEM.

Look at that face in the mirror. Whatever you think of it, it looks far more youthful and attractive than it would if you did not run, and all without the bother and expense of Botox or a chin lift. It is axiomatic that an improved appearance leads to higher self-esteem.

4. IT MAKES YOU MORE CONFIDENT.

Runners set goals, and they accomplish them; this builds confidence. What does running a 100-mile ultra have to do with turning a one-dollar bill into a one hundred–dollar bill right before a person's eyes? Nothing, except that the success Oz Pearlman achieves in his running naturally fuels success in other areas of his life. This is true for all who run.

5. IT RELAXES YOU.

Before a workout you feel tense, anxious, edgy. Afterward, the stress disappears, at least for the moment. And if you're feeling stressful about your running, it's a sure sign you're overdoing it. "Running should be a relief from stress, a way to help cope with it, not another added stress," says runner Bob Glover, and he's right.

6. IT TEACHES PERSEVERANCE.

Anyone who, in John L. Parker Jr.'s gritty phrase, runs regularly "over hill and dale out in the middle of nowhere, spit freezing on your goddamn chin" is teaching himself perseverance and discipline, two unglamorous but essential ingredients of a successful and productive life.

7. AND, OH YES, IT BRINGS SATISFACTION AND, AT TIMES, JOY.

Running and exercise are the best things to happen to mental and emotional health since the invention of anti-depressants. Since we began with Mr. Burfoot, let's end with him: "What do I get from running? Joy and pain, good health and injuries, exhilaration and despair. The sunrise and the sunset."

SNOB ASIDE

Another word about Burfoot, the longtime *Runner's World* editor who won Boston in 1968. His PR for the marathon is 2 hours, 14 minutes, 29 seconds. If you'd like to see him, go to the Manchester 5-Mile, the annual Thanksgiving Day road race in Connecticut. He has run it every year for more than fifty years and won it nine times.

THE WAY TO ENLIGHTENMENT

IT'S ON FOOT, BY WAY OF THE RUNNING ROAD.

The English author and runner Adharanand Finn describes runners as being "one of the special people, who have chosen a path of dedication and commitment." He could have added, enlightenment.

Running is mobile meditation. The thoughts you have when vigorously pumping your arms and legs as your heart races along with them can lead you into unexpected areas having less to do with the body and more to do with the mind and soul. Sound pretentious? Not to the following people.

Alberto Salazar. The Nike Oregon Project coach and elite marathoner in his day is a devout Catholic who repeats the Lord's Prayer and the rosary to himself when he runs long distances, and he feels that every runner does the same, whether they are religious or not. "I think every committed runner prays in her own way while she's moving," he said. "Something in the act of running, in the heat and rhythm and dance of your stride, connects you to the spirit."

Herb Elliott. Elliott was the Mo Farah or Hicham El Guerrouj of his time, a glorious Australian middle-distance runner who won gold in the 1,500 meters at the 1960 Rome Olympics. He spoke elo-

quently about how running connected him to the things of the spirit. He believed that tuning into the beauty and rhythms of the natural world made him a stronger competitor. "Poetry, music, forests, oceans, solitude—these were what developed enormous physical strength," he said. "I came to realize that spirit, as much or more than physical conditioning, had to be stored up before a race."

Joyce Carol Oates. The novelist and short story writer is a runner—and quite obsessed with it at times, as she admitted in a piece in the *New York Times*. While living in Detroit, she said, "I ran compulsively; not as a respite for the intensity of writing but as a function of writing." Feeling blocked, she'd go for a run, and when she returned she'd be unblocked. These runs around the city led to her breakthrough novel, *Them*, which won a National Book Award and launched her massive literary career. "In running," she wrote, "'spirit' seems to pervade the body; as musicians experience the uncanny phenomenon of tissue memory in their fingertips, so the runner seems to experience in feet, lungs, quickened heartbeat, an extension of the imagining self."

Wordsworth, Coleridge, Shelley, Thoreau, Whitman, Dickens. Thanks to Oates, who, like all good writers, does her research, we can state with confidence that these grand men of letters also enjoyed the creative stimulus that accrues to those who exercise

QUOTABLE SNOB

"Running! If there's any activity happier, more exhilarating, more nourishing to the imagination, I can't think what it might be. In running the mind flies with the body, in rhythm with our feet and the swinging of our arms."

—JOYCE CAROL OATES

vigorously. Yes, they hiked or walked rather than ran, but look at the miles they covered! Dickens, unable to sleep, rambled around London in the postmidnight darkness. Wordsworth and Coleridge tramped all about the Lake District of England singing nature's praises. But the Romantics were pikers compared to Walden Pond's walking-est resident, Emerson's Transcendental buddy who spent hours every day roaming the Concord woods on foot. "Methinks that the moment my legs begin to move," wrote Thoreau, "my thoughts begin to flow."

George Sheehan. Kenny Moore once wrote that running, as an activity and a sport, had "Thoreauvian roots." Although born in Brooklyn and a lifelong resident of New Jersey, George Sheehan philosophized about running in the spirit of the New England Transcendentalists. A practicing cardiologist, he took up running in middle age, inspired by the words of the ancient Christian theologian St. Irenaeus: "The glory of God is man fully functioning." For Sheehan, running was "a monastery—a retreat, a place to commune with God and yourself, a place for psychological and spiritual renewal."

He experienced a religious epiphany while running the roads one afternoon, feeling as if he was "moving surely and effortlessly toward infinity." He wrote, "Running that day became for me, as I'm sure it has for others, a mystical experience. A proof of the existence of God."

The good doctor met His Maker in 1993; a posthumous collection of his best work, *The Essential Sheehan*, was edited by his son Andrew and published a few years ago.

DEEP THINKERS

More on the cosmic nature of running:

If one needs further proof of the metaphysical nature of running, one need only read other running writers in addition to Sheehan.

Here are quotations all taken from popular running books published in recent years. The quotes appear in either the epigraph in the front of the book or at the start of a chapter. Not only do they show what deep thinkers runners are, they indicate that runners like to read books, itself a sign of great taste, intelligence, and breeding.

"When the divine is looking for you, that's a pretty powerful force."

—Prem Rawat, Indian-American spiritual teacher,
as quoted in Adharanand Finn's *Running with the Kenyans*

"The best runner leaves no tracks."

—Tao Te Ching, the epigraph for Christopher McDougall's *Born to Run*

"To live with ghosts requires solitude."

—Writer Anne Michaels, also from McDougall's book, introducing chapter one

"Only those who risk going too far can possibly find out how far to go."

—T.S. Eliot, the quotation that opens the second section
of Martin Dugard's *To Be a Runner*

"A guru gives us himself and then his system; a teacher gives us his subject, and then ourselves."

Writer Adam Gopnik, the introductory quote for
Kenny Moore's *Bowerman and the Men of Oregon*

"If you can force your heart and nerve and sinew/To serve your turn long after they are gone,/And so hold on when there is nothing in you/Except the Will which says to them: 'Hold on!'"

—From Rudyard Kipling's poem *If*, which opens the
prologue of Neal Bascomb's *The Perfect Mile*

"Suffering is Optional."

—The title of the foreword for Haruki Murakami's *What I Talk About
When I Talk About Running* (It comes from a remark by a runner
overheard by the author: "Pain is inevitable. Suffering is optional.")

BELIEVERS, DENIERS, AGNOSTICS

NOTES ON THE RUNNER'S HIGH

The runner's high is like God; some believe fully whereas others say no. A third group is agnostic. Neither true believers nor outright deniers, they just haven't experienced it for themselves and until they do, they remain skeptical.

It's not surprising that runners disagree on this matter. They're not a homogeneous group; they disagree on lots of things about running

even as they generally agree on its overall merits. Nevertheless, on the subject of the runner's high, everyone seems to have an opinion.

DENIERS

Dr. Jesse Pittsley, an exercise physiologist, defines the runner's high as a state of "euphoria, a feeling of being invincible, a reduced state of discomfort or pain, and even a loss in sense of time while running." If anyone believed in this magical, exercise-induced state, you would think it would be elite runners. After all, they run the most days, log the most miles, and go the fastest, giving them more chances to feel the feeling. It doesn't seem to work this way though.

John L. Parker Jr., author of the novel *Once a Runner* who was a fine runner in the era of Frank Shorter and Marty Liquori—he ran with and against them both for the Florida Track Club—lands firmly in the no camp, mocking "that sense of euphoria commonly reported by runners, the fabled 'third wind.'" His approach is more business-like, running as a job, which probably accurately reflects the attitudes of pros and top-tier college athletes who must put in the work every day. "He ran not for crypto-religious reasons—" Parker is here describing the novel's main character but also likely himself—"but to win races . . . His daily toil was arduous, satisfying on the whole, but not the bounding, joyous nature romp described in the magazines."

QUOTABLE SNOB

A greeting card by an online e-card service takes a humorous stance on the issue: "I only get runner's high by smoking pot before I run, and then not actually running."

BELIEVERS

Save perhaps for Dean Karnazes or Kilian Jornet, no one in the entire history of the world has bounded through nature more than Yiannis Kouros, who is to ultramarathons what Wilt Chamberlain was to the bedroom: a man of godlike, record-setting conquests. A native of Greece—naturally, they cast him as Pheidippides in a sword-and-sandal biopic of the ancient Athenian—Kouros holds scores of records for twenty-four–hour runs, forty-eight–hour runs, and even six-*day* runs, held all over the world. In the late stages of, let's say a 100-miler, he experiences not only the runner's high but a complete out-of-body experience.

"It is as if I see my body in front of me," he says, describing what the sensation feels like. "My mind commands and my body follows. This is a very special feeling, which I like very much. It is a very beautiful feeling and I experience my personality separate from my body, as two different things."

Dr. Jeff Brown is an assistant clinical professor in the Department of Psychiatry at Harvard Medical School. The author of *The Runner's Brain* and other books on running, he provides clinical advice to runners as part of the Boston Marathon medical team. He, too, vouches for the existence of the runner's high, although his experience of it is far different from Kouros's. Brown sees it not as mind–body separation but rather as joining them together in a magical way.

"A runner's high is like the ultimate form of dissociation and association rolled into a single brainwave. You feel no pain, yet you are one with your body," he writes. "It's almost as if your brain has decided that hard physical labor is the best thing that has ever happened to it. [These are] magical feelings."

AGNOSTICS

Scientific research tends to indicate that yes, runners do indeed experience euphoric feelings at certain times. The National Academy of Sciences describes the runner's high as "a subjective sense of well-being some humans experience after prolonged exercise . . . a sudden pleasant feeling of euphoria, anxiolysis, sedation and analgesia." A surge of endorphins in the body is commonly thought to be the cause of these feelings; more recently scientists have suggested that they may stem from chemical compounds known as "endocannabinoids," which are produced in the bloodstream during exercise and act somewhat like marijuana in that they dull pain, provide mild sensations of pleasure, and perhaps even give you the munchies too.

Such findings, however persuasive they may be, are purely academic to runners such as Alisha Perkins, who had never experienced the runner's high and consequently viewed it with John L. Parker–like disdain. "I am sure you have heard of this elusive phenomenon before," she wrote in a blog. "Every runner talks about it." But, she continued, "I had no idea what all the fuss was about. Every time they mentioned it I played along feeling as though I was faking an orgasm."

Then Perkins, who ran track in high school, got a taste of the real thing. It occurred in Fort Myers, Florida, where she and her husband, Glen, an All-Star pitcher for the Minnesota Twins, were staying during spring training. While he was busy with his job, she was tending to their two small girls with barely a moment to herself. Finally she had had enough. After he came home from practice one day, she turned the kids over to him and went out for a run to clear her head.

She started out doing her usual 2 miles—"the amount I had determined was enough to allow me to eat chocolate and not be fat"—but on this day, because she was feeling so stressed, she decided to keep going and run 5 miles, farther than she ever had gone before. That was when she got high for the first time.

"Before those five miles I hated running," she confessed. "It felt too mundane and hard, but that was because I had never run long enough to get that euphoric feeling. The feeling makes you love running instead of loathe it."

But, she went on, "something even greater happened for me out on that day—the release and freedom of running. The release of all this pent-up anxiety that I hadn't found an outlet for until now." After her run, she said, "I entered the house feeling at ease and calm, something I hadn't felt in a very long time. I was hooked. Glen, my husband, could tell too. He saw a more relaxed, calm, easy wife—and he liked it."

THE RUNNER'S BLUES

IT'S NOT ALL HIGHS.
THERE ARE SOME LOWS, TOO.

The novelist Haruki Murakami coined a term to describe how burned out he sometimes feels about running. He called it the "runner's blues."

For Murakami, a lifelong runner who has done marathons and ultras, the blues usually grab hold of him after a big race, when he's com-

pletely worn out, emotionally and physically. In due time he hits the refresh button and gets back on the roads, pounding away.

Lots of things can cause you to have a low-down, rock-bottom case of the runner's blues. Here is a partial list:

INJURY

This is the worst, and the worst of the worst may be the dreaded condition known as patellofemoral pain syndrome—pain in the front of the knee—or posterior knee pain—pain at the back. Other ailments—plantar fasciitis, Achilles tendinitis, shin splints—are no day at the beach either. Suffering from an inflamed Achilles tendon, Joan Benoit Samuelson vividly describes the pain as being "so bad that if Scott [her husband] accidentally kicked my leg in his sleep, I would go through the sheets. I had to put on shoes just to go to the bathroom in the middle of the night. Walking barefoot was just too painful."

RECOVERY FROM SURGERY

If your injury requires surgery, as it did with Joan, it can be very depressing, especially if it is followed by a slow recovery period that drags on for weeks or months. Sometimes you can come back too fast and reinjure yourself, adding to the gloom. The best prescription is to avoid injury in the first place if you can. "It is important to fully understand the difference between pain and fatigue," says Joan. "Do not work into the pain zone."

SNOB ADVICE

Here is more advice from the former women's marathon world record holder: 1) Keep a training diary to note any changes or patterns that may have contributed to your problems; 2) Watch for early warning signs of tightness or pain; and 3) Treat injuries quickly with RICE—rest, ice, compression with elastic bandage, and elevation of the injured part.

RUNNER'S FEET

Moving away from the more serious aspects of the runner's blues, there can be no dispute that runners have the gnarliest-looking feet in the world. Black and blue toenails, puffy swollen red blisters, torn and bleeding skin under the balls of the feet, toenails separating from the skin, toenails completely detached, toes that look like they have severe frostbite. There is an easy remedy for this though: Keep your shoes on in public.

RUNNER'S NIPPLES

The nipples of runners, like their feet, are mostly hidden from view, which is partly the problem. Nipples chafe under T-shirts on cold winter days. Reflecting on the minor miseries of being a senior runner, Pete Magill recalls how in high school "my metabolism was a coal-burning furnace. I ran shirtless in winter. Splashed through the rain. These days, it's chafed thighs, runner's nipple and a post-run nap."

RUNNER'S THIGHS

This is a chafing aggravation similar to runner's nipples. Possible solutions: new shorts, longer shorts, tighter shorts, various lubricants. Running with a pillow between your thighs is probably not a practicable solution.

RUNNER'S BUTT

Bonnie Pfiester is a super-fit Florida gym owner and personal trainer who loves running and does it three times a week. But she has no illusions about what it does to her tuchus. "If you are ready to say goodbye to your backside (and I don't mean in a good way), then start running," she tells her clients. "Seriously. Have you ever seen a runner with a really great perky butt?"

RUNNER'S BODY

Adding to perky-less butt syndrome, a trim and fit female runner may not have as much, ah, amplitude in her breasts as some might desire. This is (or was) a sore subject for Rachel Toor, who was in bed with her boyfriend when he compared her body to a *Tyrannosaurus Rex*. "Big, muscular legs, scrawny, good for nothing little upper body," was how he put it as she lay next to him naked and vulnerable. "It's, you know, a runner's body." The one good thing about boyfriends is that, unlike your breasts, butt, thighs, knees, feet, and toes, you can get rid of them if they no longer serve a useful purpose.

SNOB MATCH GAME CHALLENGE
HIGHER RUNNING EDUCATION

Education is a key to life, and a key to faster running through smart training and good coaching. Virtually all of America's top distance runners have pursued their higher running education at a university. Interestingly, in the 1960s and '70s, elite runners tended to go to schools in the Northeast. Younger generations of top runners have shifted west.

Match the runner listed in the left column with the university he or she attended (see following page). The schools are scrambled, so you must find the correct answer for each runner in the list on the right. Answers on page 76 after the quiz at the end of this chapter.

Runner	School
Frank Shorter	Arizona State
Galen Rupp	Wesleyan College
Bill Rodgers	North Carolina
Joan Benoit Samuelson	Syracuse
Ryan Hall	Colorado
Meb Keflezighi	Yale
Deena Kastor	Arkansas
Kara Goucher	Bowdoin
Desiree Linden	Stanford
Kathrine Switzer	Oregon
Jack Bacheler	Miami of Ohio
Shalane Flanagan	UCLA

MUSIC, LAUGHTER, PLAY

3 OF THE KEYS TO MOTIVATION

It's no accident that so many running books, blogs, articles, and videos contain heaping portions of motivational advice. You gotta want to do it—or you won't do it. Simple as that.

Whether you're a weekend jogger or training for the Olympics, here are three of the keys to getting and staying motivated.

1. MUSIC

"I often refer to music as a legal drug," says Costas Karageorghis, a sports psychologist at Brunel University in London. An expert on how the beat and lyrics of a song can improve athletic performance, he creates playlists for elite athletes to use when they're training. He does the same thing at races and other events, pumping up the jams to get people stirred up. The right music can help you push the pace or keep you in rhythm with it, psyche you up for a race or workout, and make it seem like you're not going as hard or as long as you are.

2. LAUGHTER

The old saw about how laughter is the best medicine received scientific confirmation anew in a recent study conducted by Robin Dunbar, professor of evolutionary psychology at Oxford University. Dunbar

and his colleagues brought together a group of Oxford undergrads and showed them funny movies and videos in order to test the relationship between laughter and endorphins, those sprightly body-producing chemicals that are released during exercise and contribute to the runner's high and other sunny athletic feelings. *Voila!* The professors found what Jimmy Fallon or Melissa McCarthy could have told them from the start: A good laugh makes people feel good.

QUOTABLE SNOB

"There is a magic ingredient that keeps you motivated in just about any situation. When you find ways to have fun during your run you open the door for the right brain to take over and work its creative magic."

—JEFF GALLOWAY

3. FUN

Jeff Galloway, quoted in the Quotable Snob on this page, is a popular marathon training coach well-known for his run-walk-run philosophy. In his books and clinics, he teaches novices that slow running coupled with intervals of walking can transport them successfully over the 26.2 miles of distance running's premier event. He also believes that a little fun and play never hurt a body either.

"The marathon is primarily an endurance event," Galloway has written. "It is only secondarily a race and should not be an ordeal." Hardcore runners committed to the idea of running as an ordeal mock Galloway—and John "The Penguin" Bingham, another popular marathon coach, now retired—for advocating not running during a running race. Galloway represented the United States in the 1972 Olympics and finished eleventh in the 10,000 meters in 29 minutes 35 seconds. His road race CV includes wins at Peachtree and the Atlanta and Honolulu Marathons. In a race against his critics in his prime, Galloway would have gone past them like they were walking.

THE SNOB 365

MARK YOUR CALENDAR:
A FULL YEAR OF HOLIDAY RACES.

All runners get it. They like all the good bennies that come from running, and they like having a good time, too. And they do! (Most of the time.)

Take a look at the racing calendar the next time a major or even a minor holiday rolls around. No matter the occasion you will find runners cavorting around at races and runs like it's, well, a holiday.

NEW YEAR'S DAY

The New Year's Race is a unique 5K, 10K, and half marathon that takes place at night, on the Saturday after New Year's Day, and weaves around downtown Los Angeles. What makes it unique is that you actually see people, in Los Angeles, on foot and not in their cars. (Kidding! The area around Staples Center, Universal City Walk, and the longtime best spot to stroll and shop and hang, Santa Monica's Third Street promenade, are all user-friendly LA urban spaces for

those on foot.) The race includes another neat feature: a run through Dodger Stadium. NewYearsRace.com

MARTIN LUTHER KING DAY
"Let freedom run!" That's the theme of the MLKDay 5K, a joy-filled day at Piedmont Park in Atlanta, where runners, walkers, and people of all faiths gather to celebrate the life of Dr. Martin Luther King Jr., the civil rights leader who was a Baptist minister. "Good ole fashioned preachers," as the website says, make the scene, along with the usual promotions for races, health, and running-related businesses. One thing guaranteed to get your feet moving if the preaching doesn't: a drum line of 250 drummers pounding out the beat along the course. MLKDay5K.com

GROUNDHOG DAY
The Groundhog Marathon and Half Marathon is Grand Rapids, Michigan's answer to Punxsutawney Phil, the famous Punxsutawney, Pennsylvania, groundhog that every year predicts whether there will be six more weeks of winter, based on if he sees his shadow. In Grand Rapids, which is not far from Lake Michigan in the central part of the state, they have no illusions about escaping winter in early February. They *know* there will be snow on the ground, and possibly falling from the sky as well, so they decided to make the best of it and hold a marathon.

These Michiganders showed some real cleverness in laying out the course. Runners loop around a 4.4-mile course again and again and again (actually, six times), which represents a witty running reenactment of *Groundhog Day*, the very funny Bill Murray movie in which he relives the same day over and over. GroundHogMarathon.com

CHINESE NEW YEAR

The YMCA Chinese New Year Run is a 5K and 10K benefit run for the San Francisco Chinatown YMCA, which acts as a recreational center for teens and young people in the city. The course passes through Grant Street in the Chinatown district—a big Chinese New Year parade is held there too—and into North Beach, the Italian section of the city. A special award goes to the runner with the best costume for that year's Chinese Zodiac animal—rooster (2017), dog (2018), pig (2019). SanFranciscoChinatown.com

PRESIDENTS' DAY

The George Washington's Birthday Marathon and Marathon Relay began in 1962 during the era in which President John F. Kennedy was urging Americans to exercise more and become more physically fit—not a bad goal, even to this day. Because it takes place in the middle of winter in Beltsville, Maryland— just across the state line from the nation's capital—the marathon is a test not only of fitness but also of how much chilly weather runners can withstand. A lot, clearly, because the event—sponsored by the D.C. Runners—remains a highlight of Washington's running scene. GWMarathon.com

SNOB ASIDE

America's thirty-ninth president, Jimmy Carter, ran as many as 5 miles a day around the South Lawn of the White House when he was in office. But his dramatic collapse during a 6.2-mile Maryland road race in 1979 caused some to fear that he had had a heart attack. Not so. Recovering quickly, he handed out trophies at the post-race awards ceremonies.

ST. PATRICK'S DAY

St. Paddy's Day and Shamrock Shuffle races occur all across the United States, but none can match Chicago's Shamrock Shuffle 8K. It is the country's and perhaps the world's biggest 8K (4.97 miles) with some thirty thousand runners following in Ferris Bueller's footsteps and dancing merrily around the city, beginning and ending in Grant Park. ShamrockShuffle.com

EASTER

Some of the most charming races take place far away from big cities and attract hundreds, not thousands, of runners. One such event is the Willimantic Easter 5K Road Race, which is hosted by Willimantic, Connecticut, a picturesque village in the eastern corner of that picturesque state. They've been running this race for decades. It loops around Valley, High, and Ash Streets before ending where it begins, at St. Mary's–St. Joseph School. Afterward there is an Easter egg hunt for kids ten and under. Wearing bunny ears is optional. TheLastMileRacing.com

APRIL FOOL'S DAY

The Winner's Circle Running Club of Salisbury, Massachusetts—it's in the northeastern part of the state, close to New Hampshire—puts on the April Fool's 4-Mile Road Race. The Winner's Circle is a sports bar in town and, not coincidentally, functions as the starting point for the race, one in a series of "Will Run for Beer" events held every year in Massachusetts and New Hampshire. The Winner's Circle is also responsible for another venerable Salisbury tradition featuring lots of beer at the post-race party: the Hangover Classic on New Year's Day. Clearly, they're having some fun up there. RunTheCircle.org

PATRIOTS DAY

Let us, for the moment, ignore that other little Massachusetts event going on down the road on this day and turn our attention to the Patri-

ots Day Road Race, a Lexington 5-miler that celebrates the battles of Lexington and Concord that brought the colonists into armed revolt against the British and ushered in the Revolutionary War. Sponsored by the local Lions Club, the race is more than one hundred years old, one of the oldest in the country. When it began, in 1914, they called it the "Paul Revere Marathon." Many of the participants don patriotic gear and Revere-style tricorne hats. LexingtonLions.org

EARTH DAY

The host city for the Earth Day Run—technically, it's a whole slew of runs: half marathon, 10K, 5K run/walk, and a kids run—is Travelers Rest, South Carolina, called TR by locals. Travelers Rest got its name in the 1800s by being a way station in the Blue Ridge Mountains for hard-drinking, hard-living "drovers," or teamsters who were moving livestock across the hills to market in Greenville. The half marathon passes through Furman University in Greenville, the Swamp Rabbit Trail, and downtown TR.

CINCO DE MAYO

The organizers of these Oregon Cinco de Mayo runs—5K, 10K, half marathon—encourage everyone to have fun but *not* to complain if you have to wait in line for a post-race Lagunitas beer and Mexican food. About three thousand people participate, and even more come to watch, so it can get a little crowded in Portland's Pioneer Courthouse Square, where everything happens. "Remember, when 3,000 people all decide to wait till the last minute to pee or check their clothing, there will be a line," says the race website. "In fact any time 3,000 people do *anything*, there is probably going to be a line." TerrapinEvents.com

MOTHER'S DAY

The female-only Kansas City Express Mother's Day 5K celebrates moms by dividing the sexes—mothers, grandmothers, and daughters run, while fathers, grandfathers, and sons cheer them on from the sidelines. The host club, the KC Express, is a local running and walking club for women. MothersDayRun.com

ARMED FORCES DAY

President Harry Truman created Armed Forces Day after World War II to honor all branches of the nation's military. Previously the Army, Navy, Marine Corps, and Air Force each had a separate day. The Armed Forces Day 5K and 10K at Lake Cunningham Park in San Jose, California, honors all men and women who wear the uniform and raises money for VSSA, a support agency for veterans with service-connected disabilities. Vssainc.org

MEMORIAL DAY

Traditionally held on the Sunday of Memorial Day weekend, the Indianapolis 500 is America's greatest automotive race (sorry, Daytona fans). The 500 Festival Mini-Marathon—despite the name, it's a half— occurs earlier in May and it's a premier event leading up to the 500. Attracting thirty-five thousand runners, it has also become one of the nation's biggest half marathons, circling the storied Brickyard oval before getting the checkered flag in downtown Indianapolis. Few races can match its cheery Midwest hospitality; more than one hundred marching bands, musical acts, and spirit squads dance and sing along the way. IndyMini.com

FATHER'S DAY

Fairhaven, Massachusetts, is an old New England fishing town about 50 miles south of Boston. It sits at the mouth of the Acushnet River on Buzzards Bay near Cape Cod, across the water from New Bedford, the one-time stomping grounds of Melville's Captain Ahab. (If you have time when you're there, go see the New Bedford Whaling National Historic Park on the waterfront, which features sailing vessels, buildings, and artifacts from that era.) Settlers first came to the area in 1653, and 322 years later the very first Fairhaven Father's Day Road Race went off with a handful of old salts leading the charge. Now the second-biggest road race on the South Coast, it attracts thousands every year. FairhavenRoadRace.com

CANADA DAY

A shout-out to America's neighbor to the north. Canada Day, a national holiday, celebrates the 1867 legislative act that united the vast provinces into a single country. Pacific Spirit Regional Park in Vancouver hosts this Run Canada Day 10K and 5K. A West Coast port city with gorgeous natural features, Vancouver bears many similarities to Seattle, Portland, and San Francisco, and like those cities has a vibrant running scene. RunCanadaDay.com

FOURTH OF JULY

When you think of giant, flag-waving, flag-carrying, red-white-and-blue Independence Day road races, one pops to mind above all: the Peachtree Road Race in Atlanta. Its zillions of runners—it is the biggest race in the country, even bigger than the New York City Marathon—carry on with a rambunctious independent spirit worthy of a great nation's birthday. The first race in 1970 began humbly, in an old Sears parking lot on Peachtree Street. Of the 150 runners who started, 110 finished. Local racing lore proudly refers to those hardy finishers as the "Original 110." AtlantaTrackClub.org

LABOR DAY

In a video on the website for the Macon Labor Day Road Race, a silver-haired woman runner with a sweet Southern drawl talks about what it's like to run this 5K and 10K in Macon, which is about 90 miles south of Atlanta on I-75. "I started running when I was forty-eight, and I'm still running," she says. "I enjoy the competition. I enjoy see-

> "Think of taking a shower. That's just the point. It's so natural. It's the same with running. Just like a shower, running is part of my daily life."
>
> **—NINA KUSCSIK, women's distance running pioneer**

ing friends. I just enjoy it." No finer testament to a race or running in general has been spoken. MaconTracks.org

CONSTITUTION DAY

Constitution Day honors that fine September day in 1787 when the Founding Fathers signed and ratified the US Constitution, the law of the land. Universities, schools, and other institutions hold events around the country to mark the day, including this Constitution Day Fun Run held at the University of Texas in Arlington. It's on the Sunday before the official date. NCPA.org

COLUMBUS DAY

The Columbus Day 5K Road Race takes place in Oak Bluffs—or OB, as the locals call it—on Martha's Vineyard, the tony island retreat in the waters off the Massachusetts coast. Everyone meets on Lake Avenue at the Wesley House, a restored Victorian hotel built in the grand style that sits regally on the harbor. The course flows around East Chop—more local argot: a *chop* is a residential neighborhood—with splendid views of West Chop, Vineyard Sound, and OB. MVOL.com

HALLOWEEN

Of the countless Halloween races there are to choose from, the best hook belongs to the Sleepy Hollow Halloween 10K of Sleepy Hollow,

New York. Readers of Washington Irving and his short story "The Legend of Sleepy Hollow" need hardly be reminded that Sleepy Hollow was where the terrified Ichabod Crane rode away on horseback from the ghoulish specter that was chasing him, the Headless Horseman. Fox made a television series about it, and Johnny Depp did his Ichabod turn in a movie also loosely based on the story. Two key landmarks in the original Irving tale—the burial ground and the Old Dutch Church—still exist, and the run goes past them. But be on alert for the smashed pumpkins! RivertownRunners.org

VETERANS DAY

November 11 commemorates Armistice Day, the day in 1919 when the fighting stopped in World War I. In 1954, after two more bloody American conflicts, the holiday became Veterans Day to honor veterans of all wars. The idea for the National Veterans Day Run came about when a group of runners and volunteers attended the Chicago Marathon on 10-10-10 (October 10, 2010). Thinking that it'd be cool to hold a race on 11-11-11 as a way to honor veterans, the first National Veterans Day Run took place on that day the following year. The series has since expanded nationally; host cities include Los Angeles, Las Vegas, Fort Worth, and Oklahoma City. VeteransDayRun.com

THANKSGIVING

There are excellent places to trot with the turkeys all over America, but one of the best, oldest, and most popular Thanksgiving Day races is the 4.78-mile Manchester Road Race in Manchester, Connecticut. It's Amby Burfoot's favorite race and fifteen thousand people run with him every year before going home to turkey and stuffing. One of Burfoot's boyhood heroes was the late Dr. Charlie Robbins, who also ran Manchester fifty times and won it twice. He sometimes ran barefoot. www.ManchesterRoadRace.com

CHRISTMAS AND THE HOLIDAYS

Reindeer Runs are as ubiquitous as Turkey Trots. This Reindeer Run, at Lake Harriet in southwest Minneapolis, combines a 5K run and walk with a children's toy drive. Salvation Army representatives pass out coffee and hot chocolate, both of which are in heavy demand, it being December in Minnesota. The road you run should be clear, but everywhere else it's snow, snow, snow. And cold, cold, cold. Bundle up. ReindeerRun.com

BOXING DAY

Boxing Day is the day after Christmas, a traditional holiday in Canada. For nearly a century the residents of Hamilton, Ontario—about 40 miles south of Toronto on Lake Ontario—have celebrated Boxing Day by strapping on their shoes and going running. Organized by the Hamilton Harriers, these 4- and 10-milers also pay tribute to Harold Webster, a gritty Hamilton native and steelworker who suffered hard luck in his running career but emerged to become one of Canada's best early marathoners. BoxingDayRun.Ca

NEW YEAR'S EVE

What better way to bring in the New Year than in the city where the ball drops? Purists may argue that the NYRR Midnight Run is technically a New Year's *Day* run, since it goes off at the crack of midnight, but that's a quibble. Safely away from the mobs in Times Square, this 4-mile Central Park romp boasts a festival-like atmosphere with dancing, frivolities, and explosions of fireworks as the clock strikes twelve. Many runners write New Year's resolutions on their bibs in an expression of hope and optimism for what is to come. Nyrr.org

ODE TO FREEDOM

7 WAYS THAT RUNNING SETS YOU FREE

Running is music and laughter and play and the freedom to wear silly costumes. It fills you with the joys of movement and gives you a way to express yourself.

Granted, the freedom you feel when you run is not like being freed after spending nearly three decades in a South African prison like Nelson Mandela (who, BTW, was a cross-country runner in high school and college. He jogged in his cell and in the prison yard to stay fit and mentally alert.) But it *is* a form of freedom, and runners from the front of the pack to the back feel this emotion keenly. Here are seven reasons why:

1. YOU'RE OUT OF YOUR ORDINARY CLOTHES.

And there are fewer of them. Different shirt, no tie, no business-y blouse or suit, running shoes not dress shoes, no heels, no makeup, hair not being fussed over. The whole look is different, and it's liberating.

2. YOU'RE OUT OF THE HOUSE AND OFFICE.

Home and office (or work site) are where you spend most of your day, but they're not where you run. When you run, you go other places,

outside places—around some neighborhoods, across the park, on a dirt path, over a hill.

3. YOU FEEL LIKE YOU'RE FLOATING SOMETIMES.

Many writers describe the action of feet striking pavement with words like *plod, trod, thump, pound, slap.* But runners themselves often report different feelings than these words convey. "When you're hitting it right," says Alberto Salazar, "to run feels like an effortless float." Joan Benoit Samuelson says that when she starts to struggle in a race she visualizes "positive images of training runs where I've felt myself floating."

4. IT MAKES YOU FEEL ALIVE.

When you're physically fit and on top of your game you feel like Bruno Mars in the "Uptown Funk" video. Just too damn hot. Julio, get the stretch. "It just feels free," was how Paula Radcliffe puts it. "It's when things click and I feel as though I'm running as fast as I can."

SNOB ADVICE

Paula Radcliffe would be the first to say, however, not to push too hard to feel as effortless as she looks when she's running. Let it come to you, don't overdo it or strain. Radcliffe knows whereof she speaks; she has suffered numerous injuries and setbacks in her record-setting world championship career.

5. RUNNING IS SIMPLE.

It's not tangled up in a web of rules and restrictions like so much of ordinary life. You get up, you get out, you run. You sweat, you come back, you take a shower. Results are clear and simple. Check your watch. That tells you how you've done, if you care to pay attention to it. And you may not.

6. IT STIRS UP MEMORIES OF CHILDHOOD.

"Townspeople used to peek out their windows and wonder, 'Why does that boy run all the time?'" recalled Joe Henderson in *Starting Lines*, his memoir about growing up in rural Iowa and what a *rara avis* he was to be a long-distance runner in the 1950s and '60s. For Henderson, a well-known author and marathon coach now in his seventies, running evokes the more carefree days of his past, and he is hardly alone in this regard.

7. YOU DEFY THE DICTATES OF TIME AND AGE.

This is an old adage of running—how it changes your view of aging, since it is an advantage to turn forty or fifty or sixty, where you can now compete against others in your age category who are older. Your times may be faster than theirs and give you a leg up in age-group racing. Still, nobody outruns Father Time forever. But at least you can go the distance with him.

HOW TO CREATE A SUCCESSFUL MANTRA

In the classic children's story "The Little Engine That Could," the train makes it over the mountain by repeating over and over to himself, "I think I can, I think I can."

The determined little locomotive *thought* he could, and he did. This is the underlying rationale for a mantra, an inspirational saying used by runners to help keep them going and climb their personal mountains. But how do you create a really good mantra, one that truly does the job? A few suggestions:

Keep it short and punchy. If it's too long to be written on your arm or a bracelet, it's probably not right. Considering that you may be somewhat out of your mind with pain and fatigue when you call on your mantra, best not to get too verbose. Grete Waitz's was as simple as it gets: "Just keep going."

Do what works for you. The ultra runner Jessica Goldman relies on phrases such as: "Today is my day." "I am strong. I am tough." "I can dig deeper. I'm almost there." She uses different mantras for different parts of a race, depending on how far she has to go. Another runner, Tara Anderson, repeats to herself: "Lighter, softer, faster, relaxer." *Relaxer* is not a word, but if it works for Tara, that is all that counts.

Get help if you need it. Mantras can be tricky things at times, and if you're having trouble coming up with just the right one for you, think about getting professional advice. A sports psychologist can help you find the perfect phrase to keep you focused and positive. There will of course be a fee for these services, but in our view it's well worth it. Money comes and goes, but a good mantra lasts forever.

Consider using an advertising slogan. If you're still having trouble coming up with the right mantra, look no further than the ad slogans of your friendly neighborhood multinational shoe corporation. adidas: "Impossible is nothing." Asics: "Stop at Never." Brooks: "No matter what your pace, run happy." "Every run is a good run." "Feed me." "Left. Right. Repeat." New Balance: "Keep Running." Nike: "Just do it." "Make it count." "Free yourself." "Strong is the new beautiful." Saucony: "Find your strong."

Let the Force be with you. Runner and personal trainer Amanda Brooks likes these mantras: "Stronger and stronger by the mile." "Today I'm fit. Fast. Fierce." "Do or do not. There is no try." This last is from Yoda, the giant-eared Jedi Master of *Star Wars*, which opens up a whole new realm of possibilities—mantras written by cynical Hollywood screenwriters adapting the pseudo-spiritual guise of *Star Wars* characters. Qio-Gon Jinn: "Your focus determines your reality." Gold Five: "Stay on target." Ahsoka Tano: "This is a new day, a new beginning." Chewbacca: "Uurrrrrrahhrrrrr."

Draw from the greats. More sources of potential mantra inspiration (suggested by Amanda Brooks) are the elite distance runners of today. Meb Keflezighi: "Boston strong." Desiree Linden: "Calm, calm, calm. Relax, relax, relax." Amy Cragg: "I breathe in strength, I breathe out weakness." As long as you don't get confused and breathe out strength and breathe in weakness, you should be fine.

RUNNING SNOB QUIZ #2
RUNNING SONGS

It is a commonplace among runners to have a playlist of songs that gets them up and moving to the beat. But how many of your songs actually refer to running? Test your musical IQ here. All these songs (and one band) use *run* or *running* in their name or lyrics. The beats are good too, so consider adding them to your playlist. Answers follow the quiz.

1. Run-DMC is the pioneering rap group that had the good sense to put *run* in its name. What brand of sneakers did the rappers wear in their music video "It's Tricky" and are most identified with?
   a. New Balance
   b. Nike Air Jordans
   c. adidas
   d. Puma

2. Florence + the Machine's mysterious but powerful "Dog Days Are Over" warns mothers, fathers, children, and others to "run fast" away because something menacing is coming after them. What is it?
   a. zombies
   b. tornado
   c. horses
   d. wolves

3. "Runaway Baby" by Bruno Mars also issues a warning, advising a girl to "run away" from him because he is certain to break her heart if they hook up. To what does he compare himself in the song?

    a. a midnight rambler

    b. a player who likes to play

    c. Casanova

    d. wolf in sheep's clothing

4. Running away is a popular theme of running songs. The quintessential running away song—and some would argue, still the best—is the 1961 hit "Runaway." Name the artist who cowrote and sang it. (Note: Tom Petty and the Heartbreakers paid tribute to him in "Runnin' Down a Dream.")

    a. Chubby Checker

    b. Roy Orbison

    c. Del Shannon

    d. Bobby Darin

5. The Talking Heads's "Psycho Killer" is another "running away"–themed song in the dark and ominous mode like Florence + the Machine. The Psycho Killer that people should run from is based on a famous movie killer. Who is it?

    a. Norman Bates

    b. Hannibal Lecter

    c. Freddy Krueger

    d. Patrick Bateman

6. More movie trivia: Soldiers must run, not walk, to stay alive in Credence Clearwater Revival's haunting song "Better Run Through the Jungle." In what Oscar-winning war movie was this song featured?

    a. *American Sniper*

    b. *Apocalypse Now*

    c. *Lone Survivor*

    d. *Platoon*

7. On a sunnier, less violent note, Paul McCartney's post-Beatles band, Wings, produced a fetching little ditty called "Band on the Run." In it is a character named "Sailor Sam." Which one of these characters did NOT appear in a Lennon-McCartney Beatles song?

   a. Father McKenzie

   b. Billy Shears

   c. Bungalow Bill

   d. Ruby Tuesday

8. Jackson Browne's "Running on Empty"—"I don't know where I'm running now, I'm just running on empty"—is an apt expression of how many runners feel at the end of a marathon. It also played on the soundtrack of a major movie with a running theme. Name the movie.

   a. *McFarland USA*

   b. *Marathon Man*

   c. *Forrest Gump*

   d. *Running Man*

9. Like "Running on Empty," Bruce Springsteen's "Born to Run" and "Thunder Road" are powerful and dramatic driving songs that use the concept of running to convey emotion and movement. In "Thunder Road" Springsteen sings to a girl, asking her to come away with him. What's her name?

   a. Julianne

   b. Mary

   c. Patti

   d. Lily

10. In his Motown dance classic "Twenty-Five Miles," Edwin Starr sings about how many miles he must go to get back to his baby. Although he is walking, not running, the lyrics almost seem written with runners in mind. All of the following lines appear in the song. But one of them is also in the lyrics of a Todd Rundgren

rock song about how he must *leave* his girl. Which line does double duty in both songs?

a. "Oh I got to walk on, let me tell you."

b. "I'm so tired, but I just can't lose my stride."

c. "Come on feet, start moving."

d. "Feet don't fail me now."

Answers: 1. c; 2. c; 3. d; 4. c; 5. a; 6. d; 7. d; 8. c; 9. b; 10. d

Answers to Match Game, Higher Running Education on page 55: Shorter, Yale; Rupp, Oregon; Rodgers, Wesleyan; Benoit, Bowdoin; Hall, Stanford; Keflezighi, UCLA; Deena Kastor, Arkansas: Goucher, Colorado; Linden, Arizona State; Switzer, Syracuse; Bacheler, Miami of Ohio; Flanagan, North Carolina

CHAPTER THREE

Chasing the Dream

Running is aspirational. Those who run do it for a variety of reasons, but all share a common goal: to live a healthier, more fully realized life. (And that may be the most amazing thing of all: Many of them do, because of running.) This chapter focuses on the *getting there* part of the equation—how to keep growing and improving as a runner in order to achieve your dreams.

THE RUNNERS' BANQUET

THE SNOB'S GUIDE TO
SHORTER DISTANCE RACES

What sort of runner would you like to be? Good? Better? The best? Or would you like to be someone who can simply look in the mirror and feel pleased because you're in such fine shape and health?

However you respond, it is beyond argument that entering a race can help motivate your training and get you where you would like to go. But which race, at what distance? What follows is the Snob's guide to running's grand banquet of shorter-distance races, starting with one of the most glamorous and storied events in all of sport.

THE MILE

Save perhaps for the marathon and 100-meter dash, no other running race can compare to the mile for drama, history, and larger-than-life characters. Roger Bannister, Filbert Bayi, Sebastian Coe, Hicham El Guerrouj, Herb Elliott, Kip Keino, Bernard Lagat, John Landy, Marty Liquori, Paavo Nurmi, Steve Ovett, Jim Ryun, Steve Scott, Peter Snell, John Walker, Alan Webb, and American Olympic gold medalist Matt Centrowitz are only a few of the gifted runners who have excelled at this distance. Female milers such as Mary Decker Slaney and Francie Larrieu Smith have also added their contributions.

These days though, the glory of the mile has faded somewhat. Road runners tend to view it as too short, too fast, and too tactical, which is largely why Kyle Merber loves it so much and finds it so exciting. Merber, who runs for the elite NJ-NY Track Club, is a former college and three time New York state prep mile champion. He thinks that 4 minutes or so is just "the right amount of time that no one is getting bored watching. Everyone is constantly on the edge of their seat." He and other mile enthusiasts are campaigning to bring it back as a featured distance running event in high school track—some schools have replaced it with the far more mundane 1,600 meters— and to revive public interest and appreciation for its glorious past. BringBackTheMile.com

3 FAST 1-MILERS

Fifth Avenue Mile. The top mile road race in the country, it starts near the Metropolitan Museum of Art, proceeds twenty blocks down Fifth Avenue alongside Central Park, and ends at an Apple store and the famed Plaza Hotel. What could be better than that? NYRR.org

Twin Cities Mile. The second-biggest mile road race in the country after Fifth Avenue, it courses over twelve city blocks in downtown Minneapolis. Like New York (and Santa Barbara), thousands of spectators line the streets to speed runners along. TCMEvents.org

State Street Mile. This mile, which runs slightly downhill (thus encouraging fast times), takes place in June in downtown Santa Barbara, a gorgeous Southern California coastal city with sunny Mediterranean-style weather. After the race is over, pack up some Coronas and fish tacos and hit the beach. SBMile.com

5K

The 5K has a natural appeal to novices, so much so that when blogger Lauren Fleshman told some "Dude on a Plane"—her description, and a good one—that her favorite race was a 5K, the guy immediately pegged her as a newbie. She took offense at this, complaining that "marathons seem to get all the love these days," but that she thinks the 3.1-mile distance is a good fit for everybody, not just those who are new to the roads. "The 5K is its own beast worth studying, pursuing and slaying," she argues, saying that it can be more than just a fun run or tempo run. Top runners use 5Ks as training runs to build their speed, just as they do the mile and other shorter distances.

Fleshman outlines other reasons why she thinks the 5K has advantages over, say, a marathon, such as you're "in pain for a shorter period of time," no ambulances are necessary, you save money on shoes, your weekends are not dominated by long, time-consuming runs, and finally, if you pick the right 5K with the best postrace party, you see more naked people.

5 FAB 5KS

Carlsbad 5000. The Carlsbad 5000—very cool name, BTW, sounds like a Grand Prix auto race—labels itself "the world's fastest 5K." It's definitely one of the prettiest, running along the breakers of the Pacific Ocean in Carlsbad Village north of San Diego. RunRocknRoll.com

Asbury Park Sheehan Classic. Bearing the spirit and memory of the late George Sheehan, this top-notch Red Bank, New Jersey, 5K has merged with the Asbury Park 5K to become the Asbury Park Sheehan Classic. Rumson and Red Bank, on the banks of the Navesink River, were the towns where Sheehan lived and practiced medicine. SheehanClassic.org

Las Vegas Rock 'n' Roll 5K. The same company that puts on the Carlsbad 5000 also stages this 5K (as well as a marathon and other races). We like it because it goes off on a Saturday night on the Vegas Strip. Don't miss the fountains at the Bellagio, a joyful spectacle of lights, music, and water. RunRocknRoll.com

Freihofer's Run for Women 5K. Freihofer's—they make baked goods—is a big all-women's race in Albany, New York. It has been around for decades and deservedly so. Thousands of women compete, including top names, and many clock fast times. FreihofersRun.com

Charlotte South Park Turkey Trot. While there are always runners at every race who want to run fast and win, many 5Ks—more than fifteen thousand are held every year—focus mainly on participation and fun. One such Thanksgiving Day event is the South Park Turkey Trot of Charlotte, North Carolina. It's one of the most popular running events in the state. CharlotteTurkeyTrot.com

QUOTABLE SNOB

"I run because I enjoy it—not always but most of the time. I run because I've always run—not trained, but run."

—AMBY BURFOOT

10K

Of the shorter races she runs, Joan Benoit Samuelson likes the 10K because it's "long enough to get into a rhythm and short enough not to require extraordinary endurance." Its 6.2 miles represent a speed and stamina-building test for elite runners who nonetheless can get into trouble if, feeling overly cocky, they go out too fast and don't save enough for the end.

Texas writer Brom Hoban calls it "the ideal weekend race," because it isn't over as fast as the 5K, it requires thinking and strategy, and the conditioning you need isn't nearly as tough as for a marathon. He points out that back in the 1970s, when running was starting to take off as a mass participant sport, 10Ks were by far the most popular race, whereas 5Ks hardly existed. Since then both 5Ks and half marathons have surpassed 10Ks in numbers of participants.

4 TERRIFIC 10KS

Cooper River Bridge Run. The Cooper River in South Carolina passes through Charleston Harbor on its journey to the Atlantic. At the harbor is a fabulous cable bridge that connects Charleston with neighboring Mount Pleasant. Starting in Mount Pleasant, this scenic 10K gives you the chance to run across the bridge into the historic and lovely Civil War city of Charleston. BridgeRun.com

Ukrop's Avenue Monument 10K. This is basically a straight shot, an out-and-back on the grand shopping boulevard of Richmond, Virginia, the one-time capital of the Confederacy and another Southern city replete with antebellum history. Monuments of Robert E. Lee and other Confederate Army heroes—as well as tennis star Arthur Ashe, a Richmond native—mark the way. SportsBackers.org

Dana Point Turkey Trot 10K. Another Thanksgiving-themed race, this one is in Dana Point in Orange County, California. One travel magazine placed it in the top three Thanksgiving race destinations in the world, which, on a planet overrun by turkey trots, is saying something. Run past the Dana Point Harbor along the cliffs of the mighty Pacific. TurkeyTrot.com

Bolder Boulder 10K. Since 1979, more than one million people have run and walked in this Memorial Day race. It starts on Walnut Street in Boulder and ends at Folsom Field, football home of the University of Colorado Buffaloes. BolderBoulder.com

WORLD'S GREATEST 7.1-MILE ROAD RACE

The Falmouth Road Race is the world's greatest 7.1-mile race and perhaps the world's greatest middle distance road race, period. Seven miles is an in-between distance for a road race—longer than a 10K but shorter than a 15K and more than half the length of a half marathon. You won't find many on your local racing calendar, and you certainly won't find any like Falmouth, which began when a local bartender named Tommy Leonard was sipping a cold one and had the idea of staging a foot race between two bars in the area—the Captain Kidd in Woods Hole, where he worked, and the Brothers Four in Falmouth Heights. The distance was a little over 7 miles and the course ran along the water.

Running has many health and fitness benefits, but it also has a long and proud tradition of drinking, of which Falmouth can claim a part. Leonard's alcohol-fueled inspiration occurred in 1972, and the next year the first annual Woods Hole to Falmouth "marathon," as it was called then, set off with less than one hundred runners. A college student on summer vacation won the inaugural event, and the grand old man of Massachusetts racing, Johnny Kelley, participated.

The August race quickly became the hottest ticket of the Cape Cod and New England racing season—"almost shorthand for summer," in Alberto Salazar's words. Salazar won it twice in those early years. So did Frank Shorter. Bill Rodgers won it three times in the days when he was unbeatable. Nowadays the Kenyans and Ethiopians are the ones who are unbeatable, dominating the race in recent decades. But Tommy Leonard is still around, and the race still basically follows the route he originally envisioned—from Woods Hole along Martha's Vineyard Sound to Falmouth Heights. Have another beer, Tommy. You deserve it. FalmouthRoadRace.com

SNOB ADVICE

As the distances get longer, it's human nature to press more—run longer, harder, faster. This may not always be wise. It is worth remembering the old adage known as the 10 Percent Rule—that is, not to increase your mileage by more than 10 percent over the previous week. This builds your strength gradually and helps avoid an injury that hobbles you or brings you to full stop.

JAMES JOYCE'S FAVORITE 12K
What does the Lilac Bloomsday Run have to do with James Joyce? Everything, according to its founder Don Kardong.

Kardong is one of the great American runners and marathoners of the first Running Boom, finishing fourth in the 1976 Olympic Marathon in a sparkling 2 hours, 11 minutes, 15 seconds. It has been argued, rightly in our opinion, that Kardong was cheated out of a bronze medal in that race due to the presence of East Germany's Waldemar Cierpinski, who took first and won the gold. Cierpinski, however, used dope; it has been shown that he and other East German athletes of this era received steroids as part of that country's corrupt state-sponsored sports program. If justice and fairness were to prevail, Kardong would be awarded the bronze he rightly won; Karel Lismont of Belgium, who finished third, would be moved up

to second; and Frank Shorter, the silver medalist, would receive the gold, turning him from a one-time Olympic marathon gold medalist, which is how he is described now, into a two-time Olympic gold medalist, which is what he truly is.

But we digress. Kardong, who lives in Spokane where the Bloomsday is held (he's the race director), is also a literary bloke. He compares a road race to a journey or odyssey, and so the formal name of the run combines the city's gorgeous flowering lilacs of spring—Spokane is known as the "Lilac City," and the run is always held the first Sunday in May—with the fictional character of Leopold Bloom, whose day-long odyssey around Dublin forms the central story of James Joyce's masterful *Ulysses*.

The course loops 7.46 miles around the Spokane River, and the first-ever race, won by Shorter, took place in 1977. Nearly one hundred people have run every Bloomsday since then; they are called "Perennials." BloomsdayRun.org

THE OLDEST AND LOONIEST

Begun in 1912, the Bay to Breakers in San Francisco claims to be "the oldest consecutively run annual footrace in the world." It is certainly the oldest *and* looniest, living up to the city's reputation for eccentricity and left coast wackiness. Centipedes, pink gorillas, British red-coats, bewigged men in Hooters outfits and red lips, running traffic cones, Wonder Women, naked running guys and gals (some in full body paint), and hordes of others—fifty thousand run, two hundred thousand watch—start on the bay waterfront, climb up and over Hayes Hill (California's answer to Heartbreak Hill), and glide into the finish amid the fog and dunes of Ocean Beach. It's approximately a 12K, and the sea of humanity on Hayes Hill, all those heads and bodies bobbing up and down, is truly an amazing sight. ZapposBaytoBreakers.com

IS HE, OR ISN'T HE?
MARK ZUCKERBERG
RUNS THE WORLD.

The most famous recreational miler in the world is Mark Zuckerberg, the Facebook billionaire who in 2016 ran a mile every day for 366 days and challenged users of his site to do the same. Tens of thousands of people did, led by Zuckerberg, who posted pictures of himself jogging past the Brandenburg Gate in Berlin, Gaudi's La Sagrada Familia in Barcelona, Tiananmen Square in Beijing, and other notable places.

A characteristically cynical and curmudgeonly journalist, Sage Lazzaro, noticed something odd about all those Zuckerberg pictures, however. He is smiling in every one of them.

"He is the most joyous runner I have ever seen," grumbled Lazzaro. "It's possible he has great endurance and can run for a while without getting that look of death on his face, but if you zoom in, it doesn't even look the face of someone who is moving! So is he actually running or is he—like the rest of us—just spending all of his time watching those recipe videos that automatically play when you scroll down the newsfeed?"

Despite Lazzaro's tongue-in-cheek suspicions—he also wondered if Zuckerberg was splashing water on the front of his T-shirt to make it appear that he was sweating—these pictures could not possibly have been photoshopped. Because, as has been well documented, everything that appears on the Internet is true.

WHERE TO RUN

THOUGHTS ON THE CITY,
SUBURBS, AND COUNTRY

Once a novice runner sets a training goal, such as completing a 5K or half marathon, another basic issue to be resolved is where to run. The obvious answer is, "Wherever you are. Throw open the door and go."

But what happens after you throw open that door and bravely venture outside? This brief survey offers a glimpse of the pleasures and pitfalls of running in the city, suburbs, or country.

CITY

Apart from the constant traffic, the threat of being hit by a heedless driver, the areas you must avoid due to the high crime rate and various unsavory characters lurking about, the awful choking air, the water and slush in the gutters being sprayed up at you by taxis during wet or snowy weather, the honking horns, the noise, the sirens, the sudden startling angry shouts of drivers, the urine smells in doorways, the holes and uneven surfaces of the sidewalks and streets, the overflowing stinky trash bags and bins waiting to be picked up, the crowds of shoppers and pedestrians blocking your way, and the absolute need for situational awareness at all times, running in the

city is the ultimate high. You can truly let go and feel, in Erin Beresini's phrase, "like a superhero."

Speaking of superheroes, one city phenomenon you may wish to explore is called "free running." It is a form of street acrobatics similar to Parkour in which urban athletes vault over fire hydrants, bounce against building walls, swing around light poles, and even do somersaults over objects they meet in their path. It popped into the public consciousness most dramatically in Daniel Craig's first Bond film, *Casino Royale*, when he and a gunman battled on a skyscraper that was under construction, sprinting across beams, scaling cables, and jumping through the air between giant cranes.

Then again the coffee may not have kicked in yet, and you may not be in a superhero frame of mind this morning. In which case find a nearby park with a pleasant trail and enjoy yourself amid the safety and company of other runners.

SUBURBS

Running in the suburbs offers many of the same rewards and challenges as the city, with a few added dividends. If you get up in the early morning darkness before commuting to work, you will see coyotes, skunks, and raccoons walking about and digging into trashcans looking for scraps. Early risers will also enjoy the sight of deer happily chewing away on the lush landscaping that suburbanites spend small fortunes on.

Although the suburbs are much less interesting than cities with their shops, cafes, and cultural attractions, fortunately on a run you can plug into your tunes oblivious to the rest of the world—that is, until a carful of hard-partying teens in a used Hummer blows through a stop sign and screeches past you on the street, forcing you to jump into the bushes to save your life. "What was that?" the boy behind the wheel asks in between texting his mother and pulling on a joint. "I think," his friend replies, "it was a raccoon."

COUNTRY

Nothing beats the fresh air, open spaces, and simple pleasures of running in the country, although there too one must remain forever vigilant not to be sideswiped on the narrow, poorly maintained, poorly lit roads by a Ford 650 wide-body truck with a V10 engine driven by a logger wearing a John Deere cap and sporting a neck tattoo who yells out the window, "Get a car, a**hole!" or some other brilliant Oscar Wilde–like witticism.

Being in the country can mean you're in the mountains at higher elevation, which can make the process of breathing, so vital to runners, somewhat more problematic than at sea level. Frankly, given the various challenges runners face whether they are in the country, suburbs, or city, it is sometimes a wonder they even dare to venture outside at all.

TREADMILL DETERMINATION: THE STORY OF CHRISTINE CLARK

Dr. Christine Clark had a problem, a problem not unlike what other runners experience in winter. She couldn't run outside as much as she liked. Matter of fact, most of the time the weather was so bad she had to stay indoors.

This was the winter of 1999–2000 and Clark, who is a pathologist, was living—and trying to train—in Anchorage, Alaska. The bad weather she faced there was of the most extreme kind—fierce Arctic blizzards, freezing cold, snow piled upon snow—giving her no other choice but to take her training downstairs to her basement treadmill.

That was where you could find her, hour after hour, day after day, although she always took Sunday off to be with her husband and children—this being one of the fundamental tenets of her coach John Clark (no relation), who felt strongly that runners should rest at least one day a week. She logged about 70 miles a week on the treadmill, running at various paces but never going anywhere.

Finally March rolled around and the race she was training for—the 2000 Olympic Trials Marathon for women—was set to go off on a sweltering hot Columbia, South Carolina, day. While not exactly an unknown—Clark had won marathons in Alaska and the Northwest and finished third at Twin Cities—her times hardly ranked her among the favorites, and some of her competitors did not even know who she was. Surprising everyone but herself perhaps and her coach, the thirty-seven-year-old Clark brought it home first that day in 2 hours, 33 minutes, 31 seconds, breaking her PR in the marathon by close to 7 minutes.

The media naturally focused on her treadmill training, which runners typically despise as being boring and lacking variety, which it is. But, in our view, Clark's victory was not about treadmills or training techniques; it was about self-determination and overcoming obstacles on the path to success. She had a goal, and she was going to do everything in her power to achieve it.

"If you try really hard," she says, "you're going to have a good day. And sometimes, for no reason you can account for, you have a great day." In Columbia she had a great day, becoming the only American female marathoner to qualify for the Olympic team. She finished nineteenth at the Sydney Games later that year.

NEW WAVE V. OLD WAVE

THE STARK DIFFERENCES BETWEEN OLDER AND YOUNGER RUNNERS

Running historians generally divide the history of the sport into two eras—Running Boom I and Running Boom II. The former occurred in the 1970s before tapering off; the latter began in the mid-1990s and continues to this day.

The runners of Boom I can be fairly described as Old Wave—typically aging Baby Boomers who took up the sport when they were young and are still hard at it all these years later. Boom II runners are New Wave; they tend to be Millennials and Gen-Xers who have come to it in more recent years. Like the Joggers v. Real Runners dichotomy we illustrated in chapter 1, Old Wave and New Wave have starkly different likes and dislikes, as revealed in this informative table.

SUBJECT	NEW WAVE	OLD WAVE
Average age	40	Declines to state
Never runs without ...	Listening to tunes	Look of grim determination
What you like best about running	Fun, social	Show off how fit I am for my age
Favorite thing to do at a race	Dress up	See above
Second favorite thing	Get chased by zombies, roll in mud	Curl up at finish with thermal blanket
Favorite cartoon runner	Homer Simpson "Springfield Marathon" episode	The Road Runner
Celebrity marathon hero	Oprah Winfrey	Oprah Winfrey
Social media	SnapChat	Facebook
Social media in five years	"Who knows?"	Facebook
Hook-up app	Tinder	AARP
On their playlist	"Crazy in Love" Beyonce	Eagles' "Greatest Hits"
View of Social Security	Will go bankrupt before can collect	Collecting it now
Favorite book (Again! Who would've thought?)	Running Snob	Running Snob

HURTS SO GOOD

HOW SOME RUNNERS
FEEL ABOUT PAIN

One of the constants of running is pain. It is an unavoidable fact of life if you run regularly.

Every day millions of people, in the name of fun and physical fitness, suffer aches and pains and strains (or worse) in their legs and lower extremities. If you have trouble reconciling this apparent contradiction, it may be that you just need to look at pain in a new way.

PAIN IS YOUR FRIEND.

Running being an essentially solitary act, there is only one companion you can always count on: pain. "Make friends with pain and you will never be alone," says Ken Chlouber, founder of the Leadville Trail 100, a Colorado ultra known for the Herculean amounts of pain it inflicts on its participants. The lowest point of the race is 9,200 feet elevation, the highest is 12,600. Since it fills up every year with runners hungry for the challenge, lots of people clearly agree with him.

PAIN IS A CHALLENGE.

"I like to challenge it," Paula Radcliffe says of pain, "to see how far I can push through it." Not good advice for ordinary runners, but on

the other hand, ordinary runners do not achieve the extraordinary heights that Radcliffe has in her career.

PAIN IS SPIRITUAL.

Percy Cerutty, a mega-passionate Australian distance running coach of yore (he trained 1960 Olympic gold medal miler Herb Elliott), urged his runners to live like the athlete-warriors of ancient Sparta and develop a Stoical disregard for pain. He viewed pain like a religious ascetic, as an aspect of a spiritual quest. "Thrust against pain," he counseled his flock. "Pain is the purifier. Walk toward suffering. Love suffering. Embrace it."

QUOTABLE SNOB

"Oh. My God. Ouch. Terrible."

—LANCE ARMSTRONG'S TEXT MESSAGE TO HIS WIFE AFTER FINISHING HIS FIRST MARATHON, the New York City Marathon

PAIN IS A SIGNAL.

When Alberto Salazar was young, his coaches kept telling him to go easy. He heard it so much he started to wonder, "What would happen if I responded to pain by moving into it rather than easing away, what if I regarded pain as a signal that I was doing something right, and that I should pile on more?" Pain for Salazar was a signal that he was doing something right. For lesser runners it usually means the opposite—that they're doing something *wrong* and need to back off.

PAIN HELPS YOU WIN.

More precisely, a higher tolerance for pain provides an edge over rivals. "A lot of people run a race to see who is the fastest," said

Steve Prefontaine. "I run to see who has the most guts, who can punish himself into exhausting pace, and then at the end punish himself even more." (To see how much you know about the gutsy Prefontaine, see our quiz at chapter's end.)

PAIN IS VITAL TO SUCCESS.
Writer Paul O'Neil compared a distance runner to "a man who sets out to discover the most graceful method of being hanged. No matter how logical his plans, he cannot carry them out without physical suffering." Pain and suffering are hardships, yes. But they are also necessary to achieve your goals, goes the thinking.

PAIN TRANSFORMS YOU.
Author and running coach Martin Dugard says that running changed his life, and that pain played a role in this transformation. "Pain and suffering are equally powerful aspects of running's transformational power," he writes. "That hurt is the thing that makes you feel like the day was worth getting out of bed." He even quotes Paul in his second Letter to the Corinthians on how pain made him stronger: "I delight in weaknesses, in insults, in hardships, in persecutions, in difficulties. For when I am weak, then I am strong."

PAIN IS A BLESSING.
After being bed-ridden with the flu, George Sheehan finally felt well enough to go for a run: "What I cared about first was health, and then being able to run again." As he did so he came to the realization that the pain he felt was a kind of gift or blessing, a natural byproduct of the thing he so loved doing. "Just to run and feel the sweat and the breathing and the power in my legs. To feel again what it was like to toil up hills and to push through pain."

PAIN MAKES YOU FEEL ALIVE.
Haruki Murakami feels much the same as Sheehan did. The experience of running is unlike anything else in his life, and if pain is part of

that experience, so be it. "It's precisely because of the pain, precisely because we want to overcome that pain," he writes, "that we can get the feeling of really being alive."

GUILT TRIP

COMMON FORMS OF RUNNER'S GUILT

Like pain, guilt is another challenge that runners must overcome to achieve their goals. There is no reason for runners to feel bad about engaging in such a healthful, life-affirming activity, but some do anyway.

As an aside, if you have never experienced the guilt feelings we describe here, please do not feel guilty about this. Just accept that some people have these issues and you do not. You're fine just the way you are.

FEELING GUILTY FOR NOT RUNNING

This may be the most common form of runner's guilt. For blogger and runner Stephanie Reynolds, mornings are when it hits her. "You vow to start running in the mornings," she says. "Then 5 a.m. comes along and not even a fire alarm could get you out of bed." So she sleeps in, vowing to run after work. Then the day grinds on and she's too tired to run in the evening. This makes her feel doubly guilty—for not running early or late.

FEELING GUILTY FOR TAKING A DAY OFF

Lauren Bridge asks a question many other runners would like to have answered as well: "Why is it that taking a rest day, for the well being of your body and mind can cause so much inner turmoil?" Making you churn even more is when your rest day happens to fall on a day when it's beautiful outside.

FEELING GUILTY ABOUT TAKING TIME FOR YOURSELF

Anika Yael Natori, another runner-blogger, feels guilty because the time she devotes to running is time she could be spending with her family and loved ones or getting ahead in her job. "I feel guilty when I run," she confesses. "I feel guilty when I don't run. I feel guilty all the freakin' time."

FEELING GUILTY ABOUT BEING SELFISH

When you run you're doing something for yourself—just you—and this naturally stirs guilt. But an Englishman, Andy Jones-Wilkins, urges runners to simply accept these feelings and carry on. "Accept the feelings of guilt that are inevitable," he advises. "Long distance training and racing is an inherently selfish endeavor that can eat up days, weeks and months."

FEELING GUILTY ABOUT NOT COMING BACK FAST ENOUGH AFTER AN INJURY

Laura Gorjanc Pizmoht was running 60- to 80-mile weeks when a bad case of PF—plantar fasciitis—slammed her, forcing her to take time off to heal. "And while I waited," she recalls, "I questioned myself: Is that heel pain still pain? Is it really unbearable? Maybe I can jump back to training." Eventually she did resume her normal running schedule, although others in a similar situation should be cautious. If you come back too fast after an injury, you may reinjure yourself and be forced to take still more time off. Think how guilty you'll feel then!

HE TRAINED ROGER BANNISTER.

5 LESSONS FROM A HISTORY-MAKING RUNNING COACH

Although he's mostly forgotten now, Franz Stampfl played a lead role in the most momentous drama in distance-running history. He coached Roger Bannister, the first man to break the 4-minute mile, clocking 3 hours, 59 minutes, 4 seconds on May 6, 1954.

With guys running in the 3-minute, 40-second range these days, a 4-minute mile may seem a quaint relic of the distant past. But what Stampfl taught Bannister is neither quaint nor antiquated, and these five lessons are surely relevant to any runners today who seek to push their performance to the next level.

1. THERE ARE GOOD COACHES AND BAD COACHES.

Runners are often independent, headstrong individuals who like to break away from the pack and do things on their own. Bannister, in his mid-twenties, was like that, firing his first coach after the coach ordered him to do something. When Bannister asked why, the coach responded, "Well, you do this because I'm the coach and I tell you."

Bannister went his own way after that, drawing praise from a reporter for showing up at a big meet with "no manager, no trainer, no masseur." Nevertheless, it was not until Stampfl, a middle-aged Austrian, entered the picture that the Englishman started to threaten the record.

2. A GOOD COACH WILL TELL YOU THINGS YOU MAY NOT WISH TO HEAR.

Bannister surely bridled at the things Stampfl told him, just as he did with that earlier coach. This is one of the hardest things about having a coach, especially a taskmaster like Stampfl, who told Bannister, flat out, that if he wanted to go sub-4 he needed to train harder. A coach, if he or she is honest, is going to tell you things you don't want to hear, things that aren't complimentary, things that push you out of your comfort zone.

Chris Brasher, Bannister's teammate and another Stampfl pupil, says, "It is absolutely necessary to have someone to whom you can turn, who is entirely honest with you. Who you know will not give spurious advice. This for me was my coach."

3. A GOOD COACH WON'T OVERTRAIN YOU.

Stampfl was no patsy, to be sure, yelling at Bannister, "Do it again! Harder! Faster—it is only pain!" But, as Neal Bascomb writes in *The Perfect Mile*, his account of the three-country, three-runner race to be the first to break 4 minutes—besides Bannister, the other two top threats to do it were Wes Santee of the United States and John Landry of Australia—success for Stampfl was "not about spending endless hours in training, but rather the quality of the effort."

The Austrian, who wrote a much-admired book about his coaching philosophy, *On Running*, puts it this way: "Training is principally an act of faith. The athlete must believe in its efficacy; he must believe

that through training he will become fitter and stronger." And in running there is a precise measurement for your fitness and strength. It's called a stopwatch.

4. A GOOD COACH WILL BE POSITIVE TOO.

The greatest training plan in the world means nothing if there's no buy-in from the runner who must log all those miles and do the work. Stampfl understood this and remained ceaselessly, unflaggingly, relentlessly positive, bucking up the spirits of his runners. "Your mind can overcome any sort of adversity," he told Bannister again and again, engaging in what Chris Chataway, another Stampfl runner, called "pre-race mental calisthenics."

If Chataway said he was feeling tired, Stampfl told him he was strong. If Chataway didn't know if he had it that day, Stampfl told him yes he did, yes he did. Chataway had heard these mental calisthenics many times before, but the repetition alone provided reassurance: "Just hearing someone say these things—by then I knew what he would say—was useful," he recalled.

5. A GOOD COACH CAN HELP YOU CHANGE THE WORLD— YOUR WORLD ANYHOW.

"We honestly believed that if you have a dream and you work to make it come true," said Chris Brasher, "then you really can change

the world." And they did. Brasher and Chataway both ran in the race that day at Iffley Road Track (now named after Bannister) on the campus of the University of Oxford.

Brasher went out first and fastest, setting the early pace so the man of the moment could stay on world-record time. When Brasher faltered, up stepped Chataway, who pushed it some more until Bannister—"It was as if all my muscles were part of a perfectly tuned machine," he said once, describing how he felt when he was at his best—took command on the last lap and crashed through an invisible barrier that at the time many considered to be impossible, beyond human reach. "The runner's greatest asset, apart from essential fitness of body, is a cool and calculating brain," said Stampfl. "Above all, he must have a will to win." Bannister had all that, and a good coach too.

MORE VOICES FROM THE PAST

OTHER OLD-TIME COACHES ON THE VIRTUES OF MODERATION

Many people associate the past with stricter and more authoritarian methods of coaching and training. This is not necessarily true. These great Hall of Fame track and field and distance-running coaches, all of whom have passed on, believed in training smart, not overworking, and that moderation in the pursuit of victory was a virtue.

"Rest is the greatest tonic in the world for the tired athlete, and under no circumstance should a man force himself to undergo a tiresome practice when he feels he is not up to it."

—Boyd Comstock, University of Southern California, 1924

"It is better to underwork an athlete than to overwork him."

—Clyde Littlefield, 1933, University of Texas and Olympic team coach

"The more I coached the more I became convinced that the mind, the will, the determination, the mental approach to competition are of utmost importance. Yes perhaps even more than the improvements in form and technique."

—Brutus Hamilton, University of California coach and assistant US Olympic coach for the Jesse Owens 1936 Games in Berlin

"If training means turning down food you like for a restricted diet, going to bed early when others are still enjoying themselves, and rigidly denying all the pleasantries and luxuries of life, then there is no such thing as training in track and field. Any system of training that takes the joy out of the sport is a lot of nonsense."

—Dean Cromwell, 1941 (coach of Charley Paddock, the one-time "World's Fastest Man" and Olympic gold medalist who was featured in the movie *Chariots of Fire*)

"We're not out to break records in practice, nor to use up that vital store of energy needed for the big meet."

—More from Cromwell

"Train, not strain."

—The basic maxim of Arthur Lydiard, 1960s, the New Zealand coach of three-time Olympic gold medalist and world record holder Peter Snell, and a mentor and friend of Bill Bowerman

"The best thing for my champions was also the best thing for everyone else. A good, long, Sunday romp."

—Arthur Lydiard, on why he recommended a long weekly run for all levels of runners

"Stress. Recover. Improve. That's all training is."

—University of Oregon track coach Bill Bowerman, 1970s, who always advised his runners to finish their workouts "exhilarated, not exhausted"

"The greatest improvement is made by the man who works most intelligently."

—Bill Bowerman

"Are you in this simply to do mindless labor, or do you want to improve?"

—Bowerman to a young runner who was working hard but not smart

THE SNOB 17

THE FASTEST CLUBS
AND TEAMS IN THE LAND

They're young, they're talented, and they're fast—and they want nothing to do with moderation when they're racing to win or unless and until their coach tells them to cool their jet-propelled, sound barrier–shattering, hyper-speed engines.

All right, so we're getting carried away. But only a little. Along with the elite racing divisions of the clubs listed in chapter 1, here are seventeen of the fastest teams and clubs in the land. If you're good, maybe, just maybe, you can qualify to be on one of these teams (there are restrictions, based on times, although some are attached to community clubs that welcome all abilities). Here's one piece of advice for when you try out: Fire up that engine of yours and let it burn.

CENTRAL PARK TRACK CLUB
Most of the elite clubs congregate in the West, particularly the mountain West, drawing runners who wish to train year-round or at high-elevation settings where the air is thin. But there are notable exceptions. One of them is the Central Park Track Club of New York City, founded in 1972. Focused and serious, CPTC has sent runners to the Olympics, Olympic Trials, and national club championships.

Members and those who aspire to membership meet for workouts twice weekly in Central Park, Columbia University, and East River Park. CentralParkTC.org

BROOKS BEASTS

This is the hot club in Seattle, the headquarters city for Brooks, which underwrites it. The Beasts have the best name for a running club we've seen, and they appear to have an attitude to match. "The nature of the Beasts [is] fast," says its website. "It's the one thing that unites our team of middle distance track runners. That, and a fluorescent yellow kit."

One of the top Beasts you'll see in that yellow kit is Nick Symmonds, a two-time Olympian in the 800 meters who says his running style can best be described by the title of the movie *Die Hard: With a Vengeance*. No shrinking violet, he has spoken out about what he sees as unfair endorsement rules for pro athletes and Russia's treatment of gays. BrooksRunning.com

MAMMOTH TRACK CLUB

The Mammoth Track Club of Mammoth Lakes, California describes itself as "the most accomplished distance running group in the United States," and the numbers do not lie: twelve Olympians to date, two Olympic medals, two number one world rankings, dozens of national championships and records. It was founded in 2001 by superstar coaches Joe Vigil and Bob Larsen, who brought two superstars with them, Deena Kastor and Meb Keflezighi. Things clearly clicked in this High Sierra community because Keflezighi grabbed a silver medal in the Athens Olympic marathon three years later, and Kastor won a bronze.

More success followed, although Vigil, an Olympic distance running coach, has since retired from day-to-day duties. Now Kastor is president of the board of directors and runs the club with her husband Andrew. A recently completed all-weather track and field facility in Mammoth Lakes makes the future seem bright indeed. Mammoth TrackClub.com

TRF PRO

TRF Pro is the elite affiliate of Team Run Flagstaff, a community club in the high-desert Arizona community of Flagstaff. It boasts such names as Ryan Hall—a two-time Olympian in the marathon who holds the fastest American times ever recorded in the marathon (2 hours, 4 minutes, 58 seconds) and half marathon (59 minutes, 43 seconds)—and his wife Sue Hall, a national cross-country champion and top steeplechaser. Janet Cherobon-Bawcom, a native Kenyan and US Olympian in the 10,000 meters, also belongs. She and the Halls moved to Flagstaff in part because of its 7,000-foot high elevation, ideal for altitude training. Northern Arizona University is there, scenic running trails abound, and the Grand Canyon is only a short drive away. TeamRunFlagstaff.com

NORTHERN ARIZONA ELITE

NAZ Elite is another high-performance Flagstaff running club whose members include another of running's power couples: Stephanie Bruce—a top half marathoner and cofounder of Picky Bars, an energy bar—and her husband Ben Bruce—one of the best all-round distance runners in the country, who has represented the United States in track, cross-country, and the half marathon in world championship competition. NazElite.com

ZAP FITNESS REEBOK

They've got mountains in the South too, and fast runners as well. The ZAP Fitness Foundation is a nonprofit training center nestled into the mountains of western North Carolina, near the little town of Blowing Rock. (Close by is Grandfather Mountain, where they hold a popular marathon and annual Scottish Highland Games.) The center holds running camps for all ages and abilities and sponsors a team of the young and the gifted. ZapFitness.com

ASICS GTC-ELITE

GTC stands for Greenville Track Club, a four-decades-old South Carolina institution at the center of Greenville's thriving running scene. The elite wing of the club aims to place runners high in regional, national, and Olympic Trials competition. Qualifying standards are divided into A and B levels, depending on how fast you can fly. GTC-Elite.org

FURMAN ELITE

Furman University's cross-country and track team functions as a feeder program for Furman Elite, which is made up of top post-collegiate runners from Furman and other schools. Furman Elite and the university work together to provide a professional-level training and racing program. RunFurman.com

HANSONS-BROOKS DISTANCE PROJECT

Superstar runners can be found all over the country. Olympic marathoner Desiree Linden runs for Hansons-Brooks, which is based in Rochester, Michigan, not far from Detroit. Hansons-Brooks Dis-

tance Project is an Olympic development program for college and post-college runners, particularly marathoners, and it's clearly succeeding in this regard.

Brian Sell, who never won style points as a runner but got the job done anyhow, ran for the club as well as the United States in the 2008 Olympic marathon. Male runners who are in the program bunk in two homes owned by the project, while the females live in another house supplied by Brooks. The coaches are brothers Keith and Kevin Hanson, who also own running stores in Michigan. Another graduate of the project is Danny Mackey, coach of the Brooks Beasts. Hansons-Running.com.

TEAM USA MINNESOTA

Team USA is a distance running center located in Minneapolis-St. Paul. Its men and women have won two dozen national championships and competed in the Olympics from the 1,500 meters to the marathon. Competitors hail mainly from Minnesota and other Midwest states and come to the Twin Cities to train at the University of Minnesota and Augsburg College. TeamUSAMinnesota.org

NJ ★ NY TRACK CLUB

The symbol between the NJ and the NY is a star, which tells you what you need to know about this New Jersey–New York club that calls itself "the East Coast's most successful professional track and road racing team." Olympic 5,000-meters star Julie Culley trained with this group. Frank "Gag" Gagliano, formerly of the Oregon Track Club Elite and Nike Farm Team, serves as head coach and guru. NJNYTC.com

NEW YORK ATHLETIC CLUB

Founded in 1868, the NYAC is a grand institution of New York and American sports. One of its members, Thomas Burke, won two gold

medals in the sprints in the 1896 Athens Olympics, the first modern Olympic Games. Since then NYAC athletes have competed in every Olympics except the boycott year of 1980. Many of these athletes, including in track and field, have won bronze, silver, or gold medals. It has two remarkable locations where athletes and NYAC members stay, train, and play: the Manhattan House—on Central Park South in New York City—and a 33-acre Travers Island estate in Westchester County on the Long Island Sound. NYAC.org

NIKE OREGON PROJECT

Founded by Nike chairman Phil Knight and marathoner-turned-coach Alberto Salazar, this group's mission is to train American distance runners so can they once again beat the world's best, specifically the Ethiopians and Kenyans (a goal shared by all the clubs on this list). The Cuban-born, New England–raised Salazar went to Kenya to study their training methods and came away most impressed by how they handle the mental side of running. "The Kenyan runner projects an aura of almost preternatural calm, both while running and at rest," he observed.

The Portland-based Nike Oregon Project combines the latest in high-tech coaching methods with old-school inspiration. Its motto is a quote from the late Geoff Hollister, a former University of Oregon runner and promotions man at Nike: "Air in your lungs, life in your legs, wind at your back and wings on your feet." NikeOregon Project.com

TEAM RUN EUGENE

Like its Eugene neighbor, the Oregon Track Club, Team Run Eugene is a community club with a super-fast elite program. Its prep and university stars are, typical for runners, outrageously good-looking, healthy, and vibrant. TeamRunEugene.org

AMERICAN DISTANCE PROJECT

Based in Colorado Springs, the American Distance Project offers coaching, medical, nutrition, and physical therapy guidance to its athletes. One of its best runners is Betsy Saina, the Kenyan native and three-time NCAA cross-country champ at Iowa State who moved to the Rockies to train with ADP coach Scott Simmons. Among her past accomplishments: world-leading times in the 5K and 10K. American DistanceProject.com

BOULDER TRACK CLUB

The Boulder Track Club has a development team and a high-performance team. The development team, coached by two-time British Olympian Kathy Butler, consists of younger runners with potential. As they grow older and their times improve, they move up to the BTC high-performance squad. Lee Troop, a three-time Australian Olympic marathoner, coaches the latter group, having trained in the Rocky Mountain climes for years before finally moving there with his family. Two of its hot stars: American Olympian-hopeful Jonathan Grey and ultramarathoner Cassie Scallon. BoulderTrackClub.com

BOULDER RUNNING COMPANY/ADIDAS

Another Boulder club with hot-shoes talent, the Boulder Running Company—also a local running store, which is affiliated with it—

boasts a slew of talented postcollegiate cross-country runners from around the nation who have followed the path blazed by Frank Shorter and migrated to Colorado to live and train. adidas sponsors the club, as it does other clubs elsewhere. To their credit, many local running shops and the major shoe companies—adidas, Asics, Brooks, Nike, New Balance—sponsor clubs and elite teams, which likely would not exist without their financial backing and support. Brc-adidas.blogspot.com

RUNNING SNOB QUIZ #3:

PRE

Few runners have lived more dramatically than Steve Prefontaine, who died tragically at the age of twenty-four in a 1975 car crash. One of the best of his time and one of the best ever, he set a basketful of American distance-running records from the 2 mile to the 10,000 meters and remains a legend among the cognoscenti for his all-out, hold-nothing-back, push the pace from the front ethos.

But how well do you know the legend of Pre? Find out here. Answers follow the quiz.

1. The mustachioed, long-haired Prefontaine is often compared to James Dean, the 1950s movie star of *Rebel Without a Cause*, who also lived hard and died young in a car crash. Dean crashed a

Porsche. What sports car was Pre driving on the night he was killed?

a. Porsche Speedster, like Dean

b. Corvette

c. MGB

d. Mustang

2. Pre may also be compared to Paul Walker, another Hollywood actor who died too young in a fiery automobile crash. Walker starred in all of the movies listed below. Name the one that best describes Prefontaine's running style.

a. *Joy Ride*

b. *Running Scared*

c. *The Fast and the Furious*

d. *Into the Blue*

3. In keeping with his significance to the sport, two movie biopics have been made about Prefontaine. One was *Prefontaine*; the other was the more successful *Without Limits*. Name the two actors who played Prefontaine in these movies, and for bonus points match each with his respective movie.

a. Joaquin Phoenix

b. Jared Leto

c. Kevin Bacon

d. Billy Crudup

4. One of Pre's coaches was Bill Bowerman, the crusty and blunt-spoken University of Oregon track man who is quoted earlier in this chapter. Let's hear more from him. Which of these statements did Bowerman NOT make?

a. "The only way to get to Point B is to start at Point A."

b. "You run like a turkey in a plowed field."—to one of his runners

c. "Live each day so you can look a man square in his eye and tell him to go to hell."

d. "It is the illusion that we can go no faster that holds us back."

5. "The three Bills," as they have been called, coached Oregon running for much of the past century and helped turn it into a powerhouse—Bill Bowerman; Bill Hayward, who preceded him and for which Hayward Field is named; and this Bill, who also coached and mentored Prefontaine. What is this Hall of Famer's last name?

   a. Rodgers

   b. Higdon

   c. Dellinger

   d. Bellamy

6. Prefontaine bartended at a bar in south Eugene named The Paddock, now called the Old Pad. Name the NFL Hall of Fame quarterback and University of Oregon graduate who also worked there. He's now a TV broadcaster.

   a. Troy Aikman

   b. Dan Fouts

   c. Phil Simms

   d. Trent Dilfer

7. Geography time. After Pre died, the Eugene running community built a running trail in his memory, Pre's Trail, which begins in Alton Baker Park and runs alongside a river that goes through Eugene. Name the river.

   a. Willamette

   b. Columbia

   c. Klamath

   d. Deschutes

8. Steve Prefontaine made all the statements below, all memorable in their own way. But which one is the most definitive expression of who he was and what he represented to people?

   a. "The best pace is a suicide pace, and today is a good day to die."

   b. "I hate to have people back there sucking on me."

c. "A race is a work of art that people can look at and be affected by in as many ways as they are capable of understanding."

d. "To give anything less than your best is to sacrifice the gift."

9. In one of his deepest disappointments, though his effort in the race was remarkable, Prefontaine finished fourth in a fast and talented men's 5,000-meter final at the 1972 Olympic Games. Great Britain's Ian Stewart won bronze, Tunisia's Mohamed Gammoudi took silver, and one of the best distance runners ever captured gold. Who was he?

a. Steve Ovett

b. Lasse Viren

c. Sebastian Coe

d. Kip Keino

10. Of all the records held by Pre, the longest to stand was his 1972 Olympic Trials meet record for the 5,000 meters of 13 hours, 22 minutes, 8 seconds. It took forty years for an American to finally break this record. Who did it?

a. Bernard Lagat

b. Meb Keflezighi

c. Galen Rupp

d. Alan Webb

Answers: 1. c; 2. c; 3. (b) Leto, Prefontaine; (d) Crudup, Without Limits; 4. d; Kenny Moore, one of Bowerman's pupils, said that. 5. c; 6. b; 7. a; 8. d; 9. b; 10. c

CHAPTER FOUR

Dream Achieved: Marathon

The marathon is the premier event of long-distance running. Most runners who run for any length of time dream of completing one, and once they do, they forever look back on it with feelings of accomplishment and pride. Here we talk about today's marathon scene, starting with its popular little brother, the half marathon.

A HALF THAT
MAKES A WHOLE

HOW THE HALF MARATHON
OVERCAME OBSTACLES
TO INSPIRE US ALL

When it comes to feel-good stories in sports, it is hard to top the half marathon. In recent years it has grown to become the second-most popular road race after the 5K, surpassing the marathon and attracting more than two million participants every year.

Even more remarkable, it has achieved this success despite having to face a number of obstacles that would have crippled a lesser race. This short list summarizes some of the challenges it has overcome while inspiring us all.

LACK OF MYTHOLOGY

The marathon, as everyone knows, is founded upon the myth of Pheidippides—or however you spell his name; there are several variations in common use. He was an ancient Athenian military courier who acted heroically, we believe. Truth is, no one can be sure about any of it. Pheidippides may have run by himself, or formed a relay with others, or perhaps he had only limited involvement or not at all.

In any case, without getting lost in the historical weeds, let us assume for argument's sake that a man named Pheidippides actually did do what his adherents claim—run 250K (155 miles) in less than two days to ask for Sparta's help on behalf of Athens in its battle against Darius the Great and the armies of Persia; and then, after the outmanned Athens forces unexpectedly beat the Persians, running back 25 miles or so to Athens—given that all this happened a couple of millennia ago, the precise distance is a little fuzzy—to inform the citizenry of their great victory. Mythology is *very* important to the mystique of the marathon, and it is a miracle that the half marathon has been able to do so well without it.

NO ONE DIES IN A HALF MARATHON

At the end of his second run, the one to Athens, an utterly exhausted Pheidippides—and who wouldn't be, after doing a 250K ultra and a marathon in the space of a few days—arrived in the city, proclaimed the great news, "Rejoice, we have conquered"—or words to this effect; there is much dispute about this too—and immediately collapsed and died. There are no epic tales of Greeks dying at the end of half marathons, and this is a burden the event has had to bear.

LACK OF A PLACE NAME

Marathon is the name of an actual town in Greece, the site of that famous Athens v. Persia dust-up and where Pheidippides allegedly started his marathon run. There simply is no town named Half Marathon. Go ahead, check it on Google maps; it just doesn't exist.

NO IDENTIFYING LANDMARK

Even people who know next to nothing about marathons have heard the phrase "Heartbreak Hill," which is the final hill in a series of hills that runners must face, to their infinite agony, late in the Boston Marathon. This was where, in 1936, Johnny Kelley, a runner beloved

Given the historical mysteries surrounding its origins, how did the marathon grow into the remarkable event that it is today? Credit principally goes to two Frenchmen, Pierre de Coubertin and his assistant Michel Bréal, who came up with the idea for the marathon, based on the Pheidippides legend, as the dramatic finale for the first modern Olympic Games, held in 1896 in Athens. It has closed most every Olympic track and field competition since then.

by Beantown's Irish-American population, passed his chief rival in those days, Ellison "Tarzan" Brown, and took the lead in the race. As he did so he gave Brown a patronizing love tap on his back. This infuriated Brown, who roared back to retake the lead and win the marathon, breaking Kelley's heart—hence the name. Obviously there are no "heartbreak hills" in half marathon lore. What is half of a hill anyway—a mound? Heartbreak Mound just doesn't have quite the same ring to it.

NO RUNNERS NAMED TARZAN

This story only serves to remind us of another missing ingredient that half marathons have had to overcome: not enough runners with colorful nicknames.

NEGATIVE ASSOCIATIONS

No one calls the 5K a Half 10K. But the half marathon is saddled perpetually with its not-whole status and its association with phrases like half baked or half a**. Half of something, like a half moon or half dollar, is never as good as a full thing of it. Is a glass half full or half empty? Order a *demitasse* of coffee at a French café and what you get is a piddling little bit of coffee, served in a tiny cup. The half is no *demimarathon*, and yet that is how some hard-boiled runners see it.

QUESTIONS ABOUT HYPHENATION

Do you hyphenate half marathon or don't you? Well no, you don't. But early in its life when people weren't as familiar with it, the half marathon was saddled with a distracting punctuation mark in the middle of its name.

STILL MORE NEGATIVE ASSOCIATIONS

The half marathon is 13.1 miles, and we hardly need to be reminded of what the number 13 means in popular culture. Does Jason Voorhees run? If he does, the half would be his race of choice.

NOT AS MUCH TO BRAG ABOUT

Running a half marathon is a tremendous accomplishment, not half of anything but fully an achievement that people should feel proud of. Tell that to the next nonrunner you meet at a party when you say you are about to run a half marathon. "How far is that again?" he asks. Then after you tell him, he replies, "That's great. Do you think you'll ever run a real marathon? That Pheidippides was really something wasn't he?"

THE SNOB 11

HALF MARATHONS THAT STAND OUT FROM THE CROWD

It is easy to see why half marathons are so popular: They're the un-Cola. They are not the classic race distance or the standard by

THE BIRTH OF JOGGING

To locate the origins of running as a mass participation movement in America, one need not peer into the mists of antiquity. Place and date are certain: Eugene, Oregon, February 1963.

Credit as founder goes to Bill Bowerman, who went to New Zealand that summer to visit his friend and mentor, Arthur Lydiard. Like Bowerman, Lydiard was a brilliant distance-running coach and mind. When he was there, the Oregon coach saw something he had never seen before: people, in groups, running. These were casual weekend meet-ups, not training sessions, with a mix of non-athletes, young and old, jogging for fun and fitness and to come together socially in Auckland, New Zealand's capital city.

Most of the joggers—that's what they were called then—abided by Lydiard's principle of being able to talk and run at the same time. If you couldn't hold a conversation while you were jogging, you were going too fast.

Returning home, an inspired Bowerman decided to try the same thing in Eugene, inviting students and anyone else to come to Hayward Field on the U of O campus to jog around the track on a Sunday in February. He had no idea how many people would show; a couple of dozen did, that first time. Everyone jogged a mile. Word got around, and the next Sunday more people showed, including girls and women. Some seniors too. Some jogged in their street clothes, a few walked. The Sunday after that, two hundred people came.

This was all extremely new and strange and daring. No one else anywhere in the world save New Zealand was doing this: jogging together, as a form of group exercise. But not even the Kiwis had ever seen a crowd like what showed up at Hayward the next Sunday, a month after the first jogging meet-up was held—five thousand people, all running and walking around the track. Bowerman was scared someone would have a heart attack. No one did.

That was, as Kenny Moore has pointed out, the birth of the American running movement. In the years that followed, Bowerman wrote *Jogging*, an influential manual on running, and in 1968 Dr. Kenneth Cooper, a Texas physician, published his landmark best seller *Aerobics*, which inspired millions to take up regular cardiovascular exercise as a way to promote health and wellness. Now in his mid-eighties, Cooper serves as chairman of the Cooper Aerobics Center in Dallas, which he founded, and estimates that he has run more than thirty-eight thousand miles in his lifetime.

which runners and running careers are judged. Consequently they have to be a little different to stand out, and the races we've highlighted here do just that: stand out from the crowd.

For logistical and other reasons, race organizers often pair half marathons with marathons or shorter-distance races, combining them into one big event with different parts. Although our focus is half marathons, admittedly a marathon or 5K may be part of these affairs as well.

JOHNNY KELLEY HALF MARATHON

Johnny Kelley was the grand old man of Boston and Cape Cod distance running, running the Boston Marathon dozens of times and many other races until his mid-eighties, when he finally hung up his shoes. His name is tied to the legend of Heartbreak Hill and various other road race stories. Celebrate him and the beauties of New England in this May race that begins on the Hyannis Town Green and flows along past Hyannis Harbor on Cape Cod. Nearby are a memorial and museum to President John Kennedy, a Massachusetts native son who lived and vacationed there. GreatHyannisRoadRaces.com

QUOTABLE SNOB

"I love to run. This is just part of my life. It's the way I live. You put in so much effort and the rewards are so little, you might as well enjoy it and make lots of friends."

—JOHNNY KELLEY

BROOKLYN HALF

Everybody knows Coney Island. It is the site, among other attractions, of the famous Nathan's Hot Dog Eating Contest held every

year on the Fourth of July. It is also the finish for the Brooklyn Half, which has surpassed the Indianapolis Mini-Marathon as the largest half marathon in the country. Start near the Brooklyn Museum in the borough of Brooklyn and end at the Coney Island Boardwalk on the shores of the Atlantic. Check out the new rides at the amusement park, and if you're in the mood, have a foot-long. Nyrr.org

NAVY–AIR FORCE HALF MARATHON

The Marine Corps has its famous DC marathon in October; the Navy and Air Force have joined forces to hold this half marathon in town the month before. Starting near the Washington Monument, it skirts past the usual capital attractions on its way around the Rock Creek Parkway and the Potomac. Its motto—"Prepare. Execute. Achieve"—is an excellent running mantra for this race or any other. NavyHalf.com

3M HALF

This Austin half marathon advertises itself as "13.1 miles Downhill to Downtown," which may be reason enough to make the trip to Texas in January. From Stonelake Boulevard at just under 900 feet elevation, the course rises slightly at the start, then gradually drops about 300 feet until it levels off and drops again before finishing with a flourish a little above 500 feet at the Texas State Capitol. Times are fast, because, well, it's like you're running downhill. 3MHalfMarathon.com

KEY WEST HALF MARATHON

In January, lots of runners in the frigid snowbound East and Midwest escape to Key West to run this half marathon for obvious reasons: It's warm! It's sunny! Guys can run without a shirt, and everyone can shed his or her sock caps, gloves, sweatshirts, pants, and other fashionable winter running attire. Key West is a tropical island in the Florida Keys, and the course takes full advantage of this, skirting along the beaches past the water and former home of Ernest

Hemingway, who lived and wrote there. Be sure to have a taste of something with rum in it when you're there. Papa would approve. KeyWestHalfMarathon.com

DISNEY PRINCESS HALF MARATHON

This is an all-female half marathon with (to quote from the irrepressibly upbeat website) "special magical course surprises, special Princess events" and "best of all, your favorite Disney princesses [to] cheer you on your way." This February run and weekend festival at Disney Resort World in Florida also includes a "happily ever after party," the two-day glass slipper challenge, more pink than you've seen in your entire lifetime, and a few million girls and their mothers dressed up as princesses. RunDisney.com

JAZZ HALF MARATHON

St. Charles Avenue is one of the great streets of New Orleans; its old-time streetcars and fabulous Victorian mansions date back to the 1800s. The Jazz Half cruises along St. Charles on its way to Audubon Park and other downtown sights. This being New Orleans, expect to see lots of cool-cat jazz musicians along the way. Before, during, and after the race, expect to have some big fun on the Bayou. JazzHalf.com

SNOB ADVICE

Especially for first-timers, a half marathon can be as intimidating in its way as a marathon. Before a race Desiree Linden advises runners to look back on their training logs to remind themselves that they've done everything possible to prepare. "Be confident in the work you did to prepare," she says. "The race is the fun part where you get to see the hard work pay off."

RUNNER'S WORLD HALF MARATHON

Bethlehem, Pennsylvania is steel country, or what used to be steel country. It is the former HQ city of Bethlehem Steel and not far away is Allentown, made immortal by the Billy Joel song of the same name about closing all the factories down. But Bethlehem, the home for this race and festival, has lots of charm and plenty of life left in it. You run through historic neighborhoods dating back to the town's founding in 1741, and when you're done, you take in the festival on the grounds of the refurbished old Bethlehem Steel mill. Race sponsor is *Runner's World,* whose offices are in nearby Emmaus. RW.RunnersWorld.com

THE OTHER HALF; THELMA AND LOUISE HALF

Moab is a Colorado River resort town located in the remarkable red rock desert country of eastern Utah (Canyonlands and Arches National Parks are nearby). It also hosts two playful half marathons: The Other Half—in the cooler days of October—and Thelma and Louise Half Marathon—which beats the summer heat in June by going off at 6:30 in the morning. The Other Half is open to both sexes; the latter is for women only, which seems fitting considering that it is inspired by the Susan Sarandon–Geena Davis buddy flic *Thelma and Louise.* Reassuringly, runners are not required at the end to plunge to their deaths off a cliff. MoabHalfMarathon.com

TRANSAMERICA ROCK 'N' ROLL HALF MARATHON

The Golden Gate Bridge is one of the world's most beautiful bridges, a symbol of the opening of the West and an engineering master-piece. Tens of thousands of cars and trucks pass over it every day between San Francisco and Marin. Every now and then though they call a temporary halt to the traffic and let runners run across the span en masse. Such is the case with the Transamerica Rock 'n' Roll

Half Marathon. Start at Ocean Beach on the Pacific, run back and forth across the bridge where ocean meets bay, then wend your way over to the pyramid-shaped Transamerica Building downtown. North Beach and Chinatown are but steps away from the finish; both have a surfeit of good bars and restaurants for celebrating. RunRocknRoll.com

MARATHON TRAINING SECRETS

FITNESS, DIET, AND HYDRATION TIPS FROM THE GREATS OF THE PAST

One problem that casual runners have with the marathon is that the training is so hard, so rigorous, so self-denying. This belief, unfortunately, stems from a complete misunderstanding of the proper methods of marathon preparation and training.

If runners today understood how some of the greats of the past trained for the event, they would not be so intimidated by it. This knowledge might even revolutionize training methods today. Take a moment, then, to learn how our elders did it, and feel free to incorporate any of our training advice into your own prerace preparation. (BTW, none of this is made up.)

The Ancient Romans. After the decline of Greek civilization and the death of such superstars as Pheidippides, the distance-running torch passed to the Roman Empire, which also employed runners for military purposes and athletic contests. Guided by trainers, these ancients watched their diets carefully, eating dried figs, boiled grains, and cheese. They loaded up on pork as a big race drew near, thinking it would give them extra energy. To accustom runners to pain, slaves were hired to flog their bare backs with rhododendron bushes.

Snob's training advice: Try "the other white meat" for a change. Also, buy some rhododendrons at the florist. Then feel your partner out to see if he or she is interested in creative role-play as a slave.

Insights from the 1600s. Jumping ahead to the 1600s, the leading fitness experts of the time believed that a runner could run faster without his spleen to weigh him down. This theory was based on the ideas of Galen, an ancient Roman physician who thought the spleen stored many of the foul humors or toxins in the body. Whereas Roman athletes drank liquids to purify themselves, some European runners of this period opted to have their spleens removed surgically. The only thing that prevented this tactic from becoming more widespread was the high percentage of athletes who never got off the operating table after surgery.

Snob's training advice: Talk to your doctor. Surgical techniques have advanced greatly since those primitive times, and many people today lead healthy and normal lives without a spleen or even a kidney. As unusual as this approach may seem at first blush, it may be worth considering if it can bring you a new marathon PR.

Captain Barclay. Although the name sounds like a brand of rum or scotch, Captain Barclay was a real person—a Scottish runner and walker who was a leader in the pedestrian movement of the 1800s.

Pedestrianism resembled ultramarathoning in some respects, with highly motivated individuals with high pain thresholds running and walking in organized competitions over extremely long distances and time, sometimes days or a week or two. To keep in tip-top shape, Captain Barclay also advocated ridding the body of unclean toxins, undergoing routine purges, although he kept his spleen intact. His diet featured rare steak and lamb chops with stale bread and beer. After exercise, he advised, lie in bed for a half hour completely naked.

Snob's training advice: As noted previously, it is always wise to speak to your doctor before adopting any new training regimen. If you would like to follow Captain Barclay's recommendations for systematic body purges, ask your doctor to prescribe the liquid they give to patients who are about to receive a colonoscopy. It doesn't taste very good, but man, it will clean you out. And how! As for lying naked in bed after exercise, get your partner to join you and together you can administer the rhododendron therapy described in the Ancient Rome section.

Early marathoners. The night before the first modern marathon, held in Athens for the 1896 Olympic Games, the dozen or so competitors entered in the race all bunked at the same Athens B&B. Though they hailed from different countries and backgrounds, all shared similar training methods, staying up late that night drinking wine. The next morning each of them tossed back two beers apiece. One of them was Spyridon Louis, a Greek runner who, it was said, kept his strength up by downing a glass of wine during the race. Cheered on by his countrymen as he staggered through the streets of Athens, Louis took the gold and became a national hero.

Snob's training advice: Without doubt, if you're going to be a top marathoner, you need to learn how to handle your liquor. And if you don't drink and yet entertain dreams of finishing a marathon, you should probably start now.

More early marathoners. Athletic representatives from Boston came to Athens to see the marathon, and its dramatic success stirred them to return home and start a marathon in their city. Once the Americans got involved, training methods advanced rapidly. Runners were advised not to drink water before, during, or after a race. If they got thirsty, they should have whisky or brandy. One marathon pioneer, according to writer David Davis, trained on "protein shakes of raw eggs and sherry." Another took amphetamines and strychnine in small doses to boost performance.

Johnny Hayes, the New York City Irishman who won the 1908 Olympic marathon in London—the year it became 26.2 miles; it was 25 in Athens—showed how vital a good diet is to distance-running success. On the morning of his triumphant London run, he had what was described as a "light breakfast" of toast, tea, and steak.

Snob's training advice: Stay away from water, because, as the French always say, never drink anything that fish swim in. And never run and drink alcohol on an empty stomach. Be sure to have a sirloin or T-bone steak beforehand. That will set you up for the miles to come.

More advice from the French. We can always learn from the French, who are of course renowned for their athletic prowess. One such athletic role model was a marathoner named Gerard Cote, who was actually French Quebecois not a Frenchman, but same difference. He won the Boston Marathon four times, the last time in 1948. As he crossed the finish line for that race and reporters besieged him with questions, he brushed them all away with Gallic aplomb. "Gentlemen, gentlemen," he said, quieting them. "One beer. One cigar. Then we talk about the race, eh?"

Snob's training advice: Think about adding a tobacco habit—cigars are far more distinguished than cigarettes, but you be the judge—to an intense training regimen of beer, wine, whisky, brandy, steak, stale bread, figs, cheese, and rhododendron bushes.

Bill Rodgers and Grete Waitz. Contemporary runners may dismiss Cote and the others as belonging to the discredited past, but more recent marathoners of note have likewise relied on unusual training and dietary approaches. Bill Rodgers—four firsts at Boston, four in New York—slathered mayonnaise on his pizzas and ate forkfuls of peanut butter dipped in bacon bits. He enjoyed Corn Pops—he would smear peanut butter on the edge of his bowl and mix it in with the cereal—and Diet Pepsi.

Waitz liked to treat herself too, albeit with different kinds of food than Rodgers. On the night before her first appearance at the New York City Marathon, she and her husband Jack shared a luxurious meal at a Manhattan restaurant. For dinner she had a shrimp cocktail, baked potato, filet mignon, and ice cream, and the two of them split a nice bottle of red wine.

This was 1978 and the Norwegian-born Waitz, who had just turned twenty-five, had never been to New York before, and although she was an accomplished middle distance runner, had never run a marathon. Nor, as she admitted later, did she know the first thing about carbo-loading. She had never even heard of it. Nonetheless the next morning she went out and ran the boroughs of New York in a world-record time of 2 hours, 32 minutes, 30 seconds. It was the first of what would be nine New York City wins.

Snob's training advice: If you too would like to win New York City and set a world record, be sure to follow all these training tips. Verbatim, without exception.

BLOCK THAT METAPHOR!
DESCRIBING THE WALL

Another intimidating aspect of a marathon is The Wall, the Category Five hurricane that blows away runners at around the 20-mile mark of the race.

Wait. Did we just use a metaphor to describe a metaphor? Yes we did, which puts us in good company with other writers and runners attempting to convey how it feels to be so physically and emotionally drained that you almost cannot bear to take another step forward.

For Dick Beardsley, however, the image that came to mind was not that of a wall; it was an elephant in a tree. "It felt like an elephant had jumped out of a tree onto my shoulders and was making me carry it the rest of the way," he says, describing how his body felt in the later stages of his first marathon. Elephant or no, at least he tried to put words to the feeling, which Sara Latta, in an academic research paper on The Wall, was hard pressed to do.

"It evades easy definition," she writes, "but to borrow from Supreme Court Justice Potter Stewart's definition of obscenity, you know it when you see it—or hit it." Warming up as she went along, Latta did dip her toes in the metaphorical waters with this literary passage: "Some runners say it feels as if their legs had been filled with quail shot, like the stomach of Mark Twain's unfortunate jumping frog of Calaveras County."

No one had to warm up novelist Benjamin Cheever, who compares The Wall to an automobile and a gun in the same sentence: "Then it was just as if I were a car and the fan belt had gone, just as if somebody had shattered my engine block with the .357 Magnum Clint Eastwood had introduced to the public in *Dirty Harry*. And no, I didn't feel lucky. This was the wall."

This awful moment stirred bloody, fatalistic emotions in runner Erin Wyner as well. "I crashed and burned and hit the wall in my first marathon," she vividly recalls. "It was a mindless struggle, a death march to the end."

The gifted marathoner and writer Kenny Moore will not go that far though. It's not a death march, it's not even like touching a hot stove with your hand. "It's not the pain of a burning stovetop," he writes. Instead "it feels like weight that can't be borne, panic

that can't be controlled. At that moment, two paths open. You can press on and do well. Or you can back off, regroup and try to catch up."

Some years ago Moore was running alongside his friend Frank Shorter in the first marathon Shorter ever ran. When they reached the 20-mile point, Shorter hit The Wall big-time. It was like an elephant had jumped on his back, or someone had shot him with quail shot, or Dirty Harry's pistol, and he was suddenly locked in a zombie-like death march to the end. In any case, he felt *bad*. Burning with pain, he asked the one question that every marathoner would like to know: "Why couldn't Pheidippides have died here?"

THE SNOB 15

GREAT MARATHONS, GREAT MARATHON STORIES

Every marathon has thousands of stories—the stories of the runners, their families, the volunteers everywhere doing their jobs, and the spectators all along the course.

An entire book could not hold all the stories, well and completely told, of a single marathon. Here are fifteen short stories about fifteen marathons.

FRED AND GRETE
He was born Fishl Lebowitz, a Romanian Jew who escaped the Holocaust as a boy and later emigrated to the United States. "There is no

DON'T BE LIKE ROSIE.

It is a given that you're not supposed to cheat; you're taught that as a child, and your conscience and various authority figures over the years—teachers, pastors, employers, the Tax Man—reinforce this message.

So how do you explain Rosie Ruiz then?

She made marathon history at the 1980 Boston Marathon by winning a race she never ran. The Cuban-born New Yorker entered at Kenmore Square, just past the 25-mile point, and jogged the rest of the way to Copley Square, becoming the first woman to finish and being declared the winner by confused race officials. She sat on the victory stand with men's champion Bill Rodgers, who actually did run the race, and they crowned her as they did him with a laurel wreath. She also dined on beef stew, the traditional meal of Boston winners.

Many do not realize that Ruiz had to cheat just to get into Boston, and her qualifying race was the previous year at New York City, where her official recorded time was 2 hours, 56 minutes, 29 seconds. This was a lie too, as she rode the subways for much of the race and tricked officials there as well.

Even how she got into New York was a cheat. She told the Achilles Track Club, of which she was not a member, that she had brain cancer. The club kindly gave her a medical exemption that enabled her to enter the race. Whereas in New York she finished far enough back in the women's field not to arouse suspicion, in Boston her scheme succeeded all too well, and much to her surprise, she came in first and shared the podium with Rodgers, who had no idea who she was.

About a week later he found out, as did the world. Boston officials reviewed film and interviewed runners and water station volunteers, and their investigation ended with Ruiz being stripped of the title she never won in the first place. Her antics earned her a place of dishonor in the halls of running infamy and added to the lexicon: "To pull a Rosie" is synonymous with cheating in a marathon.

such thing as a stranger," he was fond of saying. "Every human being is special." Fishl changed his name to Fred Lebow and eventually became race director of the New York City Marathon.

It was Lebow who led the transformation of New York from a tiny, only-in-Central Park affair into a massive, citywide event of international status. But curiously, given his love for running, he had never run the full, five-borough race until he was almost too sick to do it. And he might not have done it all were it not for Grete Waitz.

Waitz, a former Oslo, Norway, schoolteacher who became a nonpareil distance runner, won New York for the first time in 1978, when she first met Lebow. Over the years, as she kept piling up New York victories, the two became close friends and in 1992, after he had been diagnosed with brain cancer, she helped persuade him to run the race despite his worries. He worried that he would be weak and unable to finish and that he would create a spectacle that would distract from the other runners.

None of his worries came to pass. Instead, tens of thousands of spectators lining the route recognized him and cheered him on. By his side every step of the way was Waitz, who, in an act of friendship that transcended friendship, made sure he reached the end. They walked and jogged and rested and walked and jogged and crossed the finish in well over five hours. Few who saw the pair that day were unmoved. Both these special human beings have passed on. TCSNYCMarathon.org

SOLIDARITY AGAINST TERROR
The Berlin Marathon is one of the world's best marathons, a place to go fast and set records. But after 9/11, marathon organizers did something that will last longer in people's hearts and minds than any world record.

They created a huge banner—82 feet wide by 131 feet tall—that said, "UNITED WE RUN," expressing support and solidarity with New Yorkers who were still digging out the rubble at the World Trade Center. This was in late September 2001, only weeks after the terrorist attacks that hit New York and the Pentagon and brought down a United Airlines passenger jet in Pennsylvania. Race directors and runners from around the world unfurled the banner at the start of the race and held it up above their heads.

Berlin representatives brought the sign to New York in November with the idea of having runners carry it across the Verrazano-Narrows Bridge. But high winds that day prevented that from occurring. The marathon also donated fifty thousand dollars to the NYFD. BMW-Berlin-Marathon.com

A PLACE OF HOPE

At the Oklahoma City Memorial Marathon, runners pay tribute to another painful moment in American history: the April 19, 1995, bombing of the Murrah Building in downtown Oklahoma City that killed 168 people.

The idea for the marathon originated a few years after the bombing, when two Oklahoma businessmen were on a morning run together. They started talking and decided jointly to create a race that would serve as a living tribute to those who were gone as well as provide financial assistance to the Oklahoma City National Memorial and Museum, which rose in the place where the Murrah once stood. The happy result was this marathon, which begins and ends at the memorial in the revived downtown of Oklahoma City. What was once a place of destruction is now a place of hope. OKCMarathon.com

EPOCH-MAKING EVENT

The time was 4 hours, 29 minutes, 15 seconds, which wasn't the point really. The point was this: Here was this spirited, nonathletic middle-aged woman running a marathon. That the woman was Oprah Winfrey made all the difference in the world.

Her 1994 run at the Marine Corps Marathon—which ends at the Marine Corps Memorial in Washington DC, the stirring statue of the Marines raising the flag at the Battle of Iwo Jima in World War II—is widely regarded as the epoch-making event that triggered a new wave of mass participation in running. Marathoners still look to better her time so they can say they beat Oprah. MarineMarathon.com

UP AND DOWN A MOUNTAIN

Colorado tourism agencies describe Pikes Peak as "America's mountain," and it may very well be. It is hard to think of another mountain that commands such a powerful place in the country's imagination and history. An explorer named Zebulon Pike gave it the name we call it today, and runners in the Pikes Peak Ascent have a chance to do what Zebulon never did: make it to the summit and see the awe-inspiring view of the Rockies.

But it won't be easy. The start in Manitou Springs is at 6,300 feet, and more than 13 miles of trails lie between you and the top. In mountain speak, Pikes is a "fourteener;" meaning that it's over 14,000 feet (14,110, to be precise). The Pikes Peak Marathon follows the same trail

up as the Ascent, but once you reach the top, you turn around and go back down. Good luck to all. PikesPeakMarathon.org

MOST COLORFUL NAME

The Cincinnati Flying Pig Marathon draws its name from Cincinnati history. The city in the 1800s was a meatpacking center with big cattle and hog stockyards. It became known as "Porkopolis" because of all the pigs that got loose and strayed around the streets of town. A few decades ago when Cincinnati was redeveloping its downtown area along the Ohio River, it was looking for a marketing theme; a clever designer came up with the idea of "flying pigs," which the marathon adopted as its name. The course goes by the Ohio in the footsteps of those early porcine pioneers, and pig paraphernalia—signs, decals, souvenirs, water bottles, T-shirts, costumes—abounds. FlyingPigMarathon.com

SPANNING TWO COUNTRIES

Cities often host marathons in order to promote their downtown areas and bring visitors into them. So it is with the Detroit Marathon, which puts a unique spin on the traditional business model. The course passes through two countries, traveling from Detroit to Windsor, Ontario, and back again. Entering Canada—you'll need a valid passport or other appropriate documentation to do so—you pass over the Detroit River on the Ambassador Bridge. Leaving Canada, you pass *under* the river via the Detroit-Windsor Tunnel, the only "underwater mile" in marathons, say race officials. Mile 8 is spectacular; you emerge from the tunnel back in Detroit and are greeted by cheering Stateside crowds. FreepMarathon.com

GRANDLY HISTORIC

Early in the 1900s, a man running the Yonkers Marathon had to drop out of the race because he had drunk too much whisky on the course, supplied to him by spectators who thought they were helping him.

This anecdote illustrates a) how much more we know about hydration techniques today, and b) how long they have been running marathons in the Hudson River city of Yonkers, New York. One of the oldest road races in the world, it has been receiving a freshening of late and features a new course that takes you past the river and Sarah Lawrence University, whose enthusiastic students will be on the sidelines cheering you on. If one of them offers you a hit of whisky, politely decline. TheYonkersMarathon.com

SNOB ADVICE

Proper hydration is obviously a key to performance. The University of California at San Francisco Medical Center recommends that you check your weight before and after a long run; if you lose more than 2 percent of your body weight, you're probably not drinking enough fluids. Don't wait until you feel thirsty to drink something; at that point, your body is already dehydrated.

URBAN PLEASURES

One of the pleasures of a marathon or any road race is that they often shut down or limit traffic on that day and you get to run in places where normally only cars and buses go. This is only one of the virtues of the Portland Marathon—the chance to see and experience the St. Johns Bridge, a beautiful suspension bridge over the Willamette River, in a new way. It was here that Captain William Clark camped by the side of the river in the early 1800s in his epic explorations of America with his buddy Meriwether Lewis. The race goes off in October, usually a cool and pleasant time to be on the Oregon coast. PortlandMarathon.org

TALLEST TREES

The Avenue of the Giants Marathon is the marathon of very tall trees. No marathon in the world can compete with it in this department, for these redwoods in Humboldt Redwoods State Park in Northern California are among the tallest in the world. One of them, the Stratosphere Giant, is fifteen hundred years old and more than 370 feet high. A person who hasn't done it might think that running amid these giants would make you feel small and insignificant. But it's the reverse: You feel inspired by the grandness of nature. TheAve.org

BEST COASTLINE

The Big Sur coastline of California is utterly gorgeous, and the Big Sur International Marathon held every year in April shows off a goodly piece of it. You proceed north up Highway One across the Bixby Bridge—a soul-stirring, gorge-crossing span—that, next to the Golden Gate Bridge, may be the most photographed bridge in California. This is the land Edward Weston took pictures of, and Robinson Jeffers wrote poems about. See rocky beaches, booming surf, and an occasional sea lion poking his head out of the water until you reach the finish in Carmel. Bsim.org

BEST WINE

North of San Francisco, Napa Valley is America's leading wine region, best known for its world-class Cabernet Sauvignon. The Napa Valley Marathon takes place fully in the valley, starting in the resort town of Calistoga—where you can soak in natural hot springs and mud baths—and ending in the river city of Napa. In between are miles and miles of postcard-pretty vineyards and Silverado Trail wineries such as Mumm Napa (try the sparkling), Shafer, Stags' Leap (both fine Cabernet houses), and more. NapaValleyMarathon.org

WHERE THE SUN NEVER SETS

The Anchorage Mayor's Marathon is the prosaic title for this event; the poetic name, which far better captures its magical appeal and why it draws runners from all over the planet, is the Midnight Sun

Marathon. The race and the festival that accompanies it occurs on the day of the midnight sun—in June, on summer solstice, the longest day of the year, when Alaska's biggest city almost never goes dark. On that day it gets twenty-two hours of sunlight.

The race itself swings by the waters of Cook Inlet, where you can spot eagles and moose—not your usual running sights either, to be sure. Things are happening all over Anchorage on this remarkable day when you can go for a run at midnight without a headlamp or flashlight. GoSeaWolves.com

BEST BEACHES

The Honolulu Marathon is held in December, which partially explains its perennial popularity. While the East and Midwest are boarding up for winter, on the island of Oahu it's seventy-six degrees and ridiculously pleasant. The race begins on Ala Moana Boulevard; this means "path by the ocean" in the Hawaiian language and serves as a fair description of the course, which rolls past Waikiki Beach, a touristy but still lovely beach in Honolulu with bathtub-warm turquoise waters and frolicking sea turtles. Through your shades check out glorious Diamond Head in the distance and give a nod to the statue of Duke Kahanamoku as you run by. The race is also considered a go-fast event for wheelchair flyers. HonoluluMarathon.org

QUOTABLE SNOB

"Running gives you freedom. When you run, you can go at your own speed. You can go where you want to go and think your own thoughts. Nobody has any claim on you."

—NINA KUSCSIK, marathoner

A MOMENT IN TIME

One of the most memorable moments in marathon history occurred at the Boston Marathon on Patriots' Day 1967, when race director Jock Semple tried to tear the bib off Kathrine Switzer and stop her from running in a race that was then restricted to men only. The balding Semple, in his sixties and dressed in street clothes, grabbed at Switzer, who wore No. 261 and a loose shirt and pants to avoid being detected by officials. Semple had spotted her and was angrily confronting her when Switzer's boyfriend, Tom Miller, who was running near her, stepped up and blocked him.

The strong and solidly built Miller, who had played football and threw the hammer in track and field, pushed Semple away, allowing Switzer to continue on in her quest for history. The dramatic photograph of this incident became a vivid illustration of women's attempts to gain equal rights with men in society and the forceful and intimidating efforts to stop them. Switzer, an elite runner of her time, went on to become a widely admired author and speaker and an inspiration for female and male runners.

Two words often used to describe Switzer are *class* and *dignity*, both of which she showed in 1988 when she flew to Boston to see Semple in a hospital where he lay dying. After their confrontation, the Scottish-born Semple, a former runner who had given his life to Boston sports and its marathon, had experienced a change of heart and become an advocate of women in sports and running. When Switzer appeared in the room, his face immediately brightened, and the two former antagonists—united forever by a marathon, and a moment in time—greeted each other with the warmth of old friends. Baa.org

BOSTON V. NEW YORK

WHICH IS THE BEST? YOU DECIDE.

Boston and New York have intense rivalries in baseball, basketball, and ice hockey. It seems only fitting that the two cities should also be marathon rivals.

Some say New York is the best; others argue for Boston. What do you think? Here is a handy guide for deciding which marathon beats the other.

Result: 6 to 6 with two ties. It's official! Both marathons are excellent. (What, you thought we'd choose one over the other? Seriously? We'd like to sell Running Snob *in both cities. And we'd like to be popular in Chicago too, as you'll see in the sidebar.)*

Subject	New York	Boston	Edge
History	Founded 1970	Founded 1897	Boston
Traditional day of race	First Sunday in November	Patriots Day	Boston
Bill Rodgers won	4 times	4 times	Tie
Start	Verrazano-Narrows Bridge	Hopkinton	New York
Finish	Central Park	Boylston St.	New York
Storied Landmark	Fred Lebow Statue	Heartbreak Hill	Boston
Women's record	2:22:31	2:18:57	Boston
Men's record	2:05:06	2:03:02	Boston
Dramatic ending	Tergat nips Ramaala, 2005	Duel in the Sun, 1982	Boston
Most notorious cheater	Rosie Ruiz	Rosie Ruiz	Tie
Participants	50,000	30,000	New York
Spectators	2 million	1 million-plus	New York
Culture & Neighborhoods?	Yes	Yes	New York
Most World Series titles	Yankees 27	Red Sox 8	New York

OH YES, AND DON'T FORGET CHICAGO.

The three top American marathons are Boston, New York, and Chicago. While Chicago may not be as storied as the other two, its marathon rates very well in a tale of the tape with New York or Boston. Compare its stats using the same measurements we did in the table for Boston and New York.

Founded: 1977

Traditional day of race: Sunday in October

Bill Rodgers won: Never! (But Khalid Khannouchi won Chicago four times. His 1999 win broke a world record.)

Start: Grant Park, the gorgeous civic park on the shores of Lake Michigan. Marvelous fine art to be seen at Millennium Park and the Art Institute of Chicago, which has one of the best collections of Impressionist art outside Paris.

Finish: Grant Park

Storied landmark: Two baseball landmarks of note. Runners run through Wrigleyville, not far from Wrigley Field, and they pass by US Cellular Field. The latter is home of the White Sox and the former is where the Cubs toil in the Friendly Confines.

Women's record: The Chicago women's course record, set in 2002, was also a world record for that year. Paula Radcliffe ran 2 hours, 17 minutes, 18 seconds, breaking the previous world record set the year before at yes, Chicago.

Men's record: The men's mark of 2 hours, 3 minutes, 45 seconds by Kenya's Dennis Kimetto falls short of Boston but outpaces New York. Chicago is a flat, fast course set up for records.

Dramatic ending: Any of Khalid Khannouchi's four wins could qualify. In 2002 he out-dueled Japan's Toshinari Takaoka, surging in the McCormick Place Tunnel just as he did three years earlier while setting the world record.

Most notorious cheater: Al Capone. (What, Al Capone wasn't a runner? He ran from the law, did he not? Our deepest apologies.)

Participants: 45,000

Spectators: One million-plus

Culture & neighborhoods: Yep, they got 'em in Chicago too (and thick deep dish–style pizza not thin like New York).

Most World Series titles: Come on, we're talking the Cubs and Sox here. Get real! The White Sox and Cubs each have won three world titles to date.

RUNNNG SNOB QUIZ #4

THE MARATHON

"Marathoners," wrote Liz Robbins, "push themselves to the edge of insanity and exhaustion." Please do not push yourself to insanity or exhaustion in answering the questions of this chapter's quiz on, naturally enough, the marathon. Answers follow the quiz.

1. Surprisingly, given its ancient origins, the word *marathon*—defined as a running event—did not appear in dictionaries until after a famous Olympic Games marathon that captured the attention of the world. Name the marathon.
   a. 1896 Athens, the first ever held
   b. 1908 London, the famed "showdown at Shepherd's Bush" and the first marathon to go 26.2 miles
   c. 1920 Antwerp, the first Olympics after World War I won by "Flying Finn" Hannes Kolehmainen
   d. 1936 Berlin, the stirring protest by two Korean marathoners who hung their heads on the victory stand in defiance of the Japanese occupation of their country prior to World War II
2. The official marathon distance became 26.2 miles after the King and Queen of England requested that the 1908 London Olympics race begin at Windsor Castle so they could watch the start from

an upstairs window. Previously the distance had been 25 miles. In honor of this royal contribution to the event, what do runners traditionally say when they reach the 25-mile mark?

a. "God Save the Queen."

b. "Damn queen. I wish she would've kept her mouth shut."

c. "I'll have what the Queen's having."

d. "Rule Britannia."

3. Oprah Winfrey famously ran the Marine Corps Marathon in Washington, DC in 1994, introducing a new generation to running. Three years later a prominent politician also ran the Marines Corps, finishing 30 minutes slower than Oprah did and evoking considerably less attention and admiration. Name the politician.

a. George W. Bush

b. Jimmy Carter

c. Al Gore

d. Sarah Palin

4. The first modern running boom began in 1972 when Frank Shorter ran through the streets of Munich and captured Olympic marathon gold, inspiring millions to give running a try. Two of Shorter's countrymen finished fourth and ninth in that marathon, respectively. Name them.

a. Kenny Moore, Jeff Galloway

b. Kenny Moore, Jack Bacheler

c. Jack Bacheler, Don Kardong

d. Jack Bacheler, Jeff Galloway

5. In addition to being an accomplished marathoner, Jeff Galloway is one of America's most successful marathon training coaches. If he had a bumper sticker on his car that best summed up his running philosophy, what would it most likely say?

a. "Walk, run, walk, run."

b. "Walking is for runners, too."

    c. "Slow down and run faster."

    d. "Be the turtle, not the hare."

6. John Bingham, another leading marathon coach now retired, proudly goes by a nickname that also happens to be a nemesis of Batman. What is it?

    a. The Joker

    b. Mr. Freeze

    c. The Penguin

    d. The Riddler

7. Six cities around the world host marathons that are considered to be "world marathon majors." Which of these cities hosts a world-class marathon but is NOT one of the six?

    a. Tokyo

    b. Chicago

    c. Paris

    d. London

8. Here are four top American marathons. Name the season of the year in which each occurs. Each takes place in a different season: winter, spring, summer, fall.

    a. Grandfather Mountain, North Carolina

    b. Big Sur International

    c. Houston Marathon

    d. Twin Cities

9. The Chicago Marathon was originally named after a former mayor of the city. All four of the people below have been mayors of Chicago. Which former mayor was accorded the honor?

    a. Rahm Emanuel

    b. Richard J. Daley

    c. Richard M. Daley

    d. Jane Byrne

10. And, finally, one for the English majors in the audience. Some historians believe that the creation of the Pheidippides myth came about in part because of an 1879 English poem, "Pheidip-pides," which Pierre de Coubertin almost certainly was familiar with. Name the poet who wrote this poem and probably caused de Coubertin to use Pheidippides as the inspiration for the first Olympic marathon?

a. John Keats

b. Alfred Tennyson

c. William Yeats

d. Robert Browning

Answers: 1 a; 2. a; 3. c; 4. b; 5. c; 6. c; 7. c; 8. Grandfather, summer; Big Sur, spring; Houston, winter; Twin Cities, fall; *9. B; 10. d*

CHAPTER FIVE

The Runner's Life

What defines a runner? Her heart, of course, but beyond that, what are the things of her life? Shoes, shoes, and more shoes. Food and drink—endless thoughts and cravings for food— T-shirts, gear, and off-beat races and postrace socializing that is not nearly as serious as training for a marathon or running one. Oh yes, and how to talk like a runner. All these subjects are present and accounted for in this chapter.

PASSIONATE ABOUT THEIR SHOES

IT'S NOT ABOUT FIT OR FUNCTION.
IT'S ABOUT LOVE.

Runners love their shoes the way Carrie Bradshaw loved her Jimmy Choos in *Sex and the City*. It's not merely a matter of fit or function, it's far deeper than that.

Old shoes pile up in the closets of runners long after they serve a useful purpose. Why? Because it hard to part with them. The shoes represent memories, sweet memories, of the races they've run and the people they've met and the experiences they've had that have touched their hearts in a way that few other things have in their lives.

Shoes may be inanimate objects of leather, mesh, and rubber, but they become close buddies to runners who spend so many hours and log so many miles in them. Jessie Sebor of *Women's Running* describes her feelings this way: "Once I've run a handful of workouts or races in a particular pair, I feel bonded to them. We've sweated and strained together." All this sweating and straining forms an emotional bond similar to how people feel about their dog or cat.

Martin Dugard views his shoes "as a serious monogamous relationship." And when he finds a pair that's just right for him, things get

really serious. "It won't feel like love," he tells other runners, "but something very, very close."

Powered by such feelings Dugard has come to believe that "a footwear purchase is a harmonic convergence, not a simple act of commerce." This convergence is like fate in the way it brings together young lovers. "I think the shoe finds the runner as much as the runner finds the shoe," adding that an ideal pair is when the runner's personality matches *the shoe's.*

Dugard coaches high school track, and one day he noticed one of his runners trying on a new pair of shoes. The coach knew instantly they were wrong for her. "I could see right away that the shoes were suited to someone with a different temperament. I know it sounds crazy. But I can tell when a shoe isn't right." Yes, it does sound a tad crazy, Martin, except to runners. *They get it.*

SNOB ADVICE

Dugard urges runners to make the effort to find the right shoe for them. "There is a shoe for every personality," he says, "matching an individual's aspirations with his or her physical and emotional abilities. Finding that match will make you a better runner." For the record, his match was an Asics Gel-Kayano.

The marathon coach John Bingham also talks enthusiastically about the thrill of slipping into a new pair of running shoes for the first time, describing it in terms that one might reserve for a person with whom you have just made mad passionate love. "I love buying running shoes," he glows. "I don't mean that I just enjoy the process of trying on new shoes. I mean I love buying running shoes."

Runners post pictures of their shoes online the way parents show off pictures of their babies and children. Other runners see these posts and comment on them and put up pictures of their own footwear offspring. Even if these shoes look the equivalent of Pig-Pen in *Peanuts*, they still evoke purrs of delight and affection. It may be that dirty, beat-up shoes evoke such positive responses because everyone knows they've done hard service on the roads and deserve to be recognized for it.

This is a trait shared by all members of the running tribe; they love to wax nostalgic about the shoes they've worn and loved over the years. "Although I've been running for more than 15 years and worn hundreds (yikes!) of shoes," Jesse Sebor recalls, "I think I remember every single one of them and the lessons they taught me." She carries a special fondness for her Asics Gel Cumulus, circa 1998, because they were "my first loves."

Most runners concede that, as Haruki Murakami writes, "the quality of shoes has gone way up in recent years, so shoes of a certain price, no matter what the maker, won't be all that different."

QUOTABLE SNOB

"How hard is it to make a pair of shoes? I mean, really?"

—BILL BOWERMAN, the coach and Nike cofounder whose invention of the waffle sole led to the early success of the company

Still, that doesn't mean that all shoes are created equal. The right pair of shoes can make you feel better about yourself, and this can give you a psychological lift. Continues Murakami: "Runners sense small details that set one shoe off from another, and are always looking for that psychological edge." And when they find the pair that provides that edge, all runners will agree, it's true love. And destiny.

IN PRAISE OF RUNNING SHOPS

WHERE TO FIND A RUNNING SHOE YENTA, AND MORE

If finding the right running shoe is like finding a lover, as Martin Dugard, Jessie Sabor, and so many others suggest, where do you go to find the right love match?

The answer, of course, is a running shop. There you will find a yentl, or matchmaker, operating under the guise of a store employee or clerk, who will arrange for you to meet, try on, and take home—naturally, for a fee—your ideal mate. Other services and sights you will find at a running shop include the following.

A RAINBOW WALL OF SHOES

Yes, you can find new shoes displayed at a department store or an ordinary shoe store, but not like the way they do it at a specialty running store. There you will see a glorious, heart-thumping array of shoes splashed across a single wall, in the central spot of the store, a color wheel explosion of reds and greens and yellows and purples and pinks—the women's on one side and the men's on the other, the two sexes close to each other yet kept discreetly apart as

if to prevent them from comingling in the middle of the night when the shop is closed and no one is around and producing little baby running booties.

SHOES YOU CAN ACTUALLY TRY ON BEFORE YOU BUY
Shocking, but true. You do not have to guess how these shoes will fit you, nor do they arrive at your door in a box. You are able to put these shoes on your feet prior to purchase. Mind-blowing.

RUNNING-SHOE POSTERS
There is more to see at a running shop besides shoes. Many shops have awesome shoe posters too, such as the one New Balance did some years ago to celebrate its one hundredth anniversary as a company. That poster showed eighteen different New Balance shoes, the earliest dating back to 1906 when the Boston firm was founded. That's another thing about a running shop: You can learn shoe history when you're there.

MORE JOG BRAS THAN YOU'VE EVER SEEN IN ONE PLACE BEFORE
That is, if you're a man. Women runners are used to such amazing sights and may even take them for granted. All those miraculously constructed creations reflective of the all-important job they do, lined up and hanging on a special rack, in all their different styles and colors as eye-catching in their way as the shoes on the wall. Running shops offer special fittings for women to make sure they get the right size. Cool.

OTHER RUNNERS WHO ARE MAKING AN HONEST LIVING
While a few lucky pros make a nice living from appearance fees, prize money, sponsorships, and the like, "the vast majority of professional distance runners live a starving-artist existence," explains Alberto Salazar. How they eat and pay the rent is by clerking at a

running shop. The job offers flexible hours and an understanding boss (one hopes), and lets them pursue the thing they love—to train and run. This is a win too for their customers who can draw on their expertise and experience before they make their destiny-altering shoe-buying decisions. Shopping at a specialty running store supports the runner-employees as well as the small business they work for, which is often owned by runners.

THE SNOB 10

RUNNING SHOPS THAT DO MORE THAN SELL SHOES

Many running shops, including storied ones such as the Bill Rodgers Running Center in Boston's Faneuil Hall, have closed in recent years due to online competition and for other reasons. Other shops have merged or been bought out by national chains.

In response to these economic pressures as well as the changing tastes of their customers, running shops are no longer just running shops, if they ever were. The best ones act as community centers, providing retail therapy for runners and hosting a full slate of events, runs, races, club activities, and social gatherings. Among the hundreds to choose from around the country, here are but a few examples of these busy retail running hubs.

PHIDIPPIDES

Few people in the running world wear more hats than Jeff Galloway. A former Olympic marathoner, he is best known today for his marathon training programs. He also founded Phidippides—spelled without the e before the first *i*, it must be noted—which grew to as many thirty-five stores nationally at its peak in the late 1970s. Now there are two shops in and around Atlanta, and Galloway, a busy man, still oversees the business. Phidippides.com

IRUN TEXAS

The recent history of this San Antonio store tells a story of the changing dynamics of the running-shop business. In the mid-1990s the husband and wife team of Bob and Rebecca Wallace bought the Dallas franchise of Galloway's old Phidippides chain. Concerned that their customers would have trouble remembering, let alone spelling, the name of the shop, they changed it to "Run On Dallas." Run On grew and over time added a franchise in San Antonio, where another couple, Mitch and Michele Allen, signed on as managing partners. But the Allens had to change their shop's name to iRun Texas after the Wallaces sold their Run On stores to the Denver-based Running Specialty Group chain. Running, it's fair to say, is a good deal simpler than business. iRunTexas.net

KC RUNNING AND SPORTS MEDICINE STORE

These two Kansas City–area stores—one in Missouri, the other across the border in Kansas—put a unique twist on the usual running-retail formula. They offer shoes and gear but also sports medicine products and expert therapeutic advice. Owner Mike Farmer is a trained physical therapist, and two other certified athletic trainers are on staff. KCRunningandSportsMedicine.com

SALT LAKE RUNNING COMPANY

"Marathons used to be run by lean and mean athletes," says Guy Perry, the owner of this Utah running shop, "but now they're being run by the average Joe on the street." Perry is anything but an average Joe; he is a former Nevada and Utah state track champion; veteran of numerous marathons, Ironman, and triathlon events; self-proclaimed "shoe geek"; running coach; husband; father; and cancer survivor. SaltLakeRunningCo.com

SNOB ASIDE

Running shoes figured into the life and story of Forrest Gump, played by Tom Hanks in the movie of the same name. "I've worn lots of shoes," Hanks-as-Gump said to a woman while seated on a bench waiting for a bus to come. "I bet if I think about it real hard I can remember my first pair of shoes." But Gump was wearing dress shoes, not running shoes, on that magical day when he ran so fast his leg braces broke away for good. Which may suggest that it's the runner who makes the shoes, not the other way around.

BOULDER RUNNING COMPANY

The best running shops, like the best running clubs and races, reflect their communities and the people who live in them. Founded by two elite South African marathoners, Mark Plaatjes and Johnny Halberstadt, the Boulder Running Company came of age in the late 1990s when it evolved into the center of the Boulder running community and became a model for independent retail running stores nationally. It is now part of the Running Specialty Group. BoulderRunningCompany.com

NAPA RUNNING COMPANY

The Napa Running Company in downtown Napa is tucked into a historic building that you might easily miss if you were quickly on your way to a tasting room or in your car headed to a Napa Valley winery or restaurant. But Napa has a big running scene, and this small shop is part of all of it. NapaRunningCompany.com

NAPERVILLE RUNNING COMPANY

In *Competitor*'s annual guide to American running shops, the Naperville Running Company is the only shop to win store of the year honors twice. Which begs the question: Where the heck is Naperville? The answer: in the Illinois suburbs about an hour west of Chicago. Naperville's two stores cosponsor a women's half marathon and a 5,000-meter race for fast, competitive females. RunningCompany.com

PHILADELPHIA RUNNER

Philadelphia Runner strives to be, says its website, "more than just another running store," which is what all running stores say. Nonetheless these four shops in Philly really do try to deliver on that promise, emphasizing fun and "living a healthy lifestyle. Oh and not least of all, the glorious post-workout pint with friends." We'll drink to that. PhiladelphiaRunner.com

MARATHON SPORTS

Marathon Sports is the Boston Marathon of shoe stores, opening for the first time in a redone first-floor apartment near Harvard Square in 1975. Granted that is hardly 1897, the year Boston began, but it's still quite a feat of longevity in today's brutally competitive retail climate. It labels itself "the run-walk store," and there are nearly a dozen of them in the Cambridge-Boston 'hood. One of its most popular events is a series in which people meet for a run, followed by pints at local establishments. MarathonSports.com

SAYVILLE RUNNING COMPANY

Every small business is a dream made real. Sayville Running, a specialty running store on Long Island, embodies the dreams of its two founders: Mike Nolan—a race director and marathoner—and Brendan Barrett—the former captain of Sayville High's 2000 New York state championship cross-country team. Barrett's dream, he says, was to be able to "talk about running all day and sleep late." Dream achieved. SayvilleRunning.com

FOODS FOR RUNNERS

A WHIMSICAL LOOK AT WHAT RUNNERS EAT

Because so many elite runners are skinny, there is a widespread public misconception that runners in general do not like to eat. This is not true.

Runners love to eat. *A lot.* Indeed some people run precisely because it allows them to eat whatever they want, whenever they want, including foods that are not and never will be approved by the USDA for their nutritional value. Here, then, is a whimsical food list based on what runners actually like to eat:

Sweets. This is the "you-work-hard-and-you-earned-it" category of guilty pleasures. Dark chocolate, chocolate scones, a dish of gourmet ice cream with fresh whipped cream.

Dairy. Eggnog lattes or any coffee drink with cream on top. Yogurt with fresh fruit, and don't forget to count the milk you have with your Honey Nut Cheerios in the morning.

Meat and chicken. For running snobs: a hanger steak grilled just right with a Heitz Cellars Cabernet Sauvignon. For reverse running snobs: KFC chicken and biscuits, an In 'n Out double-double cheeseburger (West Coast primarily), pizza, and a shrimp burrito.

Fruits and veggies. Butter lettuce, Romaine, arugula. Runners eat their greens, just like their mothers told them to do. Besides, rabbits like them too, and everyone knows how fast the Hare was. Fruit and veggie shakes and smoothies are good too. Next to the watch and smartphone, the blender is the most important electrical device used by runners.

Hydration. It is vital that runners hydrate properly, and they certainly do, drinking grande-size cups of tea and especially coffee, the latter ideally with an extra shot of espresso. Beer tends to reflect regional loyalties (Samuel Adams in Boston, Anchor Steam in San Francisco, Big Sky Moose Drool in Montana, and so on). Nondrinkers resort to sports drinks, Diet Pepsi, or if there's nothing else available, water.

Carbohydrates. This is the biggest food category, and thankfully there are many unhealthy items to choose from. Doughnuts are the favorite of Homer Simpson and many runners: "Doh!" Opposite Homer on the fitness spectrum are the Kenyans, who swear by a food they call *ugali*, a cornbread-like staple of their diet. If it works for them, there must be something to it. Also enjoyed by the Kenyans: boiled eggs, peanuts, lemonade.

Pasta. Finally, and forevermore, the old reliable. Angel hair, elbow macaroni, farfalle, fettuccine, lasagna, linguine, manicotti, ravioli, rigatoni, spaghetti, tortellini, ziti. A heaping plateful of whatever you fancy, topped by red or white sauce. *Mangiare!* It's all good.

THE SNOB 14

EATING AND DRINKING RACES WITH SOME RUNNING AROUND THROWN IN

Running is, for all its bumps and upsets, a pleasure. And runners have found that when they add some friends and drinking and eating into the mix, it's even more of a pleasure.

Fancy that. Runners can have their cake (or doughnuts or pizza)—and eat it too. This is the happy premise of all the eating and drinking races profiled here, a tiny taste—or swallow, if you'd rather—of all such races out there. And at the end, two drinking, eating, and running clubs of note.

KRISPY KREME CHALLENGE

This event, perhaps the most famous food race of all, began when a handful of scholarship students at North Carolina State decided to put their university education to work and see if they could run 2.5 miles across downtown Raleigh to the nearest Krispy Kreme store, eat a dozen doughnuts, and then run back the same distance to campus, all in an hour or less. They did it—the winner absolutely killed, finishing in just over thirty-four minutes—and the outpouring of national publicity they received inspired them to turn a one-time dare into an annual benefit for charity. The theme of the challenge is

"24,000 calories, 12 doughnuts, 5 miles, 1 hour," and it attracts thousands every year who try to run from campus to the Krispy Kreme and back, eat a dozen doughnuts, and do it all in under an hour. KrispyKremeChallenge.com

NEW YORK CITY PIZZA RUN

One of the great New York City dining pastimes is to buy a slice of pizza from a street vendor or shop and have it while you're standing on the sidewalk or walking. The pizza, naturally thin in the Gotham style, is so large you have to fold it over, and it's so hot you try to eat it without burning the roof of your mouth. The New York City Pizza Run celebrates this grand tradition with a 2-mile run around Alphabet City and the East Village of Manhattan. Participants must eat three slices of pizza at checkpoints along the course. No pizza eating with forks allowed. NYCPizzaRun.com

QUOTABLE SNOB

"Every night in the '80s, when I was in New York, I ate pasta with pesto. Every night, pasta and pesto. I thought that was what runners ate. Of course, I forgot the running part."

—ALLISON JANNEY, actress

RACE FOR THE BACON

When the conversation turns to the rapturous pleasures of Midwest sweet applewood smoked bacon and ham, one name and one name only comes to mind: Patrick Cudahy, the Irish immigrant who founded Patrick Cudahy premium meats and the little town of Cudahy, Wisconsin (near Milwaukee), where this 5K bacon-flavored race takes place. The start is in Sheridan Park near the statue of Cudahy, who's long gone, having died in 1919. But his influence lives on in the feast of bacon treats, dry sausage, pepperoni, ham, and deli and sliced meats that runners dine on after the race. BaconRace.com

BURGER RUN

A giant, juicy hamburger—so big, say locals, that even Guy Fieri couldn't finish it—awaits you at the end of this Kernville Canyon run. But you're going to have to earn it. In the southern Sierra Nevada mountain range east of Bakersfield, California, Kern Canyon is a big and forbidding piece of real estate, and the river that runs through it is known for its treacherous rapids. The Burger Run is a 15-mile scoot up the canyon, and the Double Burger Run—for this you get two burgers—is an out-and-back for a total of 30 miles. McNally's Fairview Lodge is where they fire up the grill for the burgers. Search online for the Burger Run.

HOT CHOCOLATE 5K

The food writer Elizabeth Dunn has described hot chocolate as "a dessert masquerading as a breakfast beverage," which means that dessert lovers will be taking a trip to paradise at Chicago's Hot Chocolate 5K, the biggest 5K race and festival in the country, with more than thirty thousand participants every year. (The event includes a 15K.) Expect a bounteous amplitude of chocolate in all its aphrodisiacal forms—hot chocolate with marshmallows, milk chocolate, dark chocolate, chocolate candy, chocolate bars, chocolate fondue, chocolate-covered pretzels, chocolate-covered bananas. HotChocolate15K.com

5K BAGEL RUN

Murray Lender can fairly be described as the father of the American bagel, calling it "the Jewish English muffin." In the 1960s he and his brothers transformed their father's company, H. Lender & Sons—now a subsidiary of Pinnacle Foods—into a bagel powerhouse, producing millions of frozen bagels that were distributed and sold across the country. People who had never tasted a bagel before had one of Murray's and found they liked it, and gradually it became a delicious staple of American cuisine. Murray's birthplace was New Haven, Connecticut, which was where the Lenders lived and built their family business. Sponsored by the Greater New Haven Jewish Community Center, this run winds through nearby Woodbridge. If you go, leave the cream cheese at home. They've got plenty. JCCNH.org

TACOS & BEER 5K

This raucous Cinco de Mayo 5K run in El Dorado Park in the Southern California city of Long Beach offers food *and* drink: two tacos and a draft beer for every adult-age participant (kids are welcome, but not to drink beer). Participants wear Mexican sombreros and serapes, and the post-race entertainment includes live mariachi music, heavy metal rock bands, a piñata-breaking party, tug-o-war, hula hoop, and your chance—at last!—to ride a mechanical bull. TacosnBeer5K.com

BOILERMAKER 15K

In the 1970s a man named Earle C. Reed, founder of the Utica Boiler Company, had an idea to put on a road race that would showcase the city of Utica, New York, where he and his family lived and where his

company and factories were thriving. He approached another businessman with his idea, F. X. Matt II, owner of another long-standing Utica institution of note, the Saranac Brewery. Matt thought it a grand idea and the "Boilermaker"—as Reed dubbed it—was born. Bill Rodgers won an early Boilermaker, and the race and its accompanying festival with its generous pourings of Saranac beer is a frothy highlight of the New York racing calendar. Boilermaker.com

DOGFISH DASH

Michael Jackson—not *that* Michael Jackson, but a different one, a widely recognized expert on beer—once called Dogfish Head "America's most interesting and adventurous small brewery." The Dogfish Dash is an interesting and adventurous race too, kicking off in Rehoboth Beach, Delaware, at the site of Dogfish Head's first brewpub. A cup of its house-made 60 Minute IPA will await you at the finish. But if you cannot quite cover 8K in that time, they've got you covered with their 90 Minute IPA. DogFishDash.Dogfish.com

HARPOON OKTOBERFEST RACE

If there were ever an event made for beer, it is this 3.6-mile Oktoberfest race sponsored by Harpoon Brewery of Windsor, Vermont. In the rambunctious spirit of the traditional German drinking frolic, there will be "nonstop oompah music," chicken dancing, cake eating contests, bratwurst, liverwurst, frankfurters, Vienna sausages, sauerkraut, and rivers of Harpoon beer. Windsor is on the Connecticut River across the border from New Hampshire. Don't forget your lederhosen. HarpoonBrewery.com

BEND BEER CHASE

The Bend Beer Chase is a team relay with beer. It covers about 70 miles in and around Bend, Oregon, a lovely little resort community in the eastern part of the state. Eastern Oregon once had active volcanoes, and you can see dormant craters around the area. A team consists of three to six people, and each person takes turns running 4 to 8 miles a leg. Relay handoffs are strategically located near local craft breweries, where you can stop and sample a few of their products if you wish. Most runners do. BendBeerChase.CascadeRelays.com

RACE TO THE TAPS

North Carolina's Race to the Taps is a most unusual and wonderful marathon. It is a marathon divided into four different races, on four different days, at four different times of the year. The first is a 5-miler in April in Asheville, followed two months later by a 6.2-miler in nearby Hendersonville, then a 7-miler in September at Black Mountain, culminating the next month with a 4- or 8-miler back in Asheville. Every race begins and ends at a craft brewery deep in the splendor of the Blue Ridge Mountains which, because the event extends from spring to fall, you get to enjoy in different seasons. RaceToTheTaps.com

SNOB ASIDE

Literary fans, please note: Asheville, North Carolina, was the hometown of Thomas Wolfe, an admired novelist of long ago and the man who coined the phrase "You can't go home again." It was the title of his best-known book. Feel free to use this as a question in any beer-drinking game of trivia you play. Asheville, as is well-known, is very big on craft beer.

HASH HOUSE HERRIERS

The Hash House Herriers famously call themselves "a drinking club with a running problem." There are hundreds of H3 chapters around the United States and world. Based on the English schoolyard game of

"Hares and Hounds," one set of runners, the Hounds, chases another set of runners, the Hares, who leave clues behind them on the trail so the Hounds can find them if they're clever. Afterward everyone meets at a pub and, fueled by cold drinks and hot comfort food, tells stories about the thrill of the chase. WorldHarrierOrganization.com

72ND STREET MARATHONING AND PASTA CLUB

A group of seven friends in New York City founded this club in the early 1970s, mainly as an excuse to go out running together in Central Park and have drinks and food after. They focused their training on the New York City Marathon, which they entered every year. Over time, though, the members grew too old to run and quit. All but Joe Mendes.

A decorated Marine Corps pilot who worked as a Wall Street investment banker until retirement, Mendes continued to run New York despite the departure of his beloved friends, and in 2005 at the age of eighty-five he became its oldest finisher. Mendes first took up the sport to stop smoking, and although it did help him ditch *that* habit, he retained a lusty taste for alcoholic beverages well into old age. His favorite: Johnny Walker Black Label.

In that 2005 race, at the 18-mile point, he and his running partner felt thirsty, so they stopped at a store for something to drink. Bottled water, sir? No thank you. For Mendes and his partner only a cold beer could quench their thirst. "Seemed like the thing to do before we hit the wall," Mendes jokingly explained to a reporter who was there too.

Runners come and go, as do running clubs and races. But like Joe Mendes, before they pass on they leave a lasting imprint.

CHEFS WHO RUN

If the usual pre-race pasta party menu—spaghetti and meatballs, garlic bread, tossed salad, perhaps a glass of house Cabernet—no longer excites you, do yourself a favor: Get to know one of these guys.

Not only are they avid runners, they can cook too. Cadge an invite to their party on the eve of a marathon, and you will have totally scored.

Richard Blais. A judge on Bravo's *Top Chef* and the winner of *Top Chef All Stars*, Blais trained at the French Laundry in Napa Valley and el Bulli in Spain—two of the world's best restaurants, although the latter no longer exists. Known for his spiky hair—his hair product, he jokes, is "equal parts duck fat and liquid nitrogen"—he has run New York in 4 hours, 17 minutes.

Dan Barber. In a Netflix documentary on Barber, food critic Ruth Reichl called him "the voice of the farm to table movement." A leading advocate of using locally sourced fresh produce and ingredients for cooking, he is chef and co-owner of Blue Hill Restaurant in Manhattan and Blue Hill at Stone Barns, on an upstate New York estate where the lean, physically fit Barber often runs.

Joe Bastianich. An Italian-American chef and TV food personality, Bastianich owns and operates a multitude of restaurants in partnership with two other famous chefs who preside over culinary empires: his friend and business associate Mario Batali and his mother Lydia Bastianich. Joe, who began running to lose weight and dropped sixty pounds, has run marathons and completed the Hawaii Ironman Triathlon.

Fabrice Hardel. The French-born Hardel is the best of the foodie-chefs who run. He cracked three hours in the first marathon he ever attempted, the Rock 'n' Roll San Diego Marathon. Since then he has logged a bunch more marathons and ultras, including one of the toughest on the planet, the Badwater 135 from Death Valley to Mount Whitney. Not bad considering his goal when he started was simply to quit a nasty smoking habit. Taste his cooking at San Diego's Westgate Hotel, where he serves as executive chef.

Gordon Ramsay. The hellacious, hell-raising, fire-breathing host of Fox's *Hell's Kitchen* is the chef-owner of a restaurant empire that stretches from his native Britain to the former colonies in the States. He trains regularly to stay fit and his best marathon finish was in London. (Food trivia: At his Maze Restaurant in London, the menu once featured what was said to be the world's most expensive pizza. Made with white truffle, it cost $145 per pie.)

NEANDERTHAL RUNNER

THE ONE-MILLION-YEAR-OLD
MAN GETS A MAKEOVER.

In the first chapter of this book, we compared a modern runner to Neanderthal Runner from one million years ago. But what if, in the manner of *Doctor Who* or *Hot Tub Time Machine*, we were able to transport Neanderthal Runner magically across time into today's world. What would that look like, and how would he do?

Obviously his whole look as a runner—gear, clothes, everything—would be woefully inadequate. As soon as he landed he would be in need of a serious makeover, starting, let's face it, with some basic hygiene.

Grooming. It's impossible not to notice that Neanderthal Runner has a rather fragrant quality about him. He also sports a woolly, bare-chested look that does have an earthy, primitive appeal. Still, it's just too much; it doesn't quite work. Let's send him to a stylist and start with a bath. Shave, wax, trim, groom. Clip the hair, beard, nose hairs, eyebrows, ear hairs, and oh god, that back hair. Don't neglect the manscaping around his package; he'll need that as well.

Shoes. Now that he's presentable, let's start with the basics. Neanderthal Runner never wore shoes, and yet he was still able to track down gazelles and other wild animals over long distances across

the African bush. This was how he hunted, in his bare feet. But frankly, how many gazelles do we need to run down today? Who eats gazelle anyway? Let's comp him a new pair of $399.99 New Balance 2040v3s with full grain leather uppers and clear rubber outsoles, and see what he can do.

T-shirt. To be a runner, he cannot own only one T-shirt or even two or three; he must have drawers and closets full of them. Fortunately this is where the running community at large can step in and help. As Kara Deschenes says, every runner has "enough race T-shirts to outfit twenty-five families of four," so there will be ample from which to choose. And once he figures how to put it on, he'll love it.

Shorts and undershorts. Neanderthal Runner is used to hanging free, which is obviously unacceptable. They'll arrest him if he tries to do that now. So let's hook him up with some technical underwear and perhaps a pair of Brooks men's Sherpa IV five-inch shorts—not too tight, made of polyester, spandex, and nylon with a moisture-proof back pocket perfect for carrying around a piece of dried bark that he can use as a comfort object or chew on if he's bored. Since he's unaccustomed to synthetics, or wearing much of anything at all, pop a tube of Body Glide into his runner's bag to prevent chafing. Just make sure he applies it to his skin and doesn't try to eat it.

For cold weather: gloves, hat, jacket, pants, hoodie, and a body-hugging long-sleeve compression shirt. On second thought, Neanderthal Runner doesn't need any of this stuff. After all, he is outdoors all year-round including winter. Hanging in caves, marking up the walls, cooking gazelles over an open fire, sporting around in animal skins and hanging free. He can handle the elements without our help.

Orthotics. Having lived his entire life up to this point in a miserable shoe-deprived state, he's surely going to need extra foot support. It's a miracle, really, that he's been able to run so far and so long without the benefit of orthotics. Can you imagine calling yourself a runner and not being on a first-name basis with your podiatrist?

Nor does he have any experience with plantar fasciitis, tendinitis, shin splints, and knees that squeak when going up and down stairs. Something is clearly wrong with the Neanderthal Runner's way of doing things. We'll straighten him out.

Electronics. In this realm Neanderthal Runner is about as on-trend as your grandmother. It's not his fault though. As everyone knows, there is absolutely no place to charge a cell phone in a cave. This primitive state of affairs manifests itself in his running too. In the bad old days, when he had to get up and go chase a gazelle, he just *did* it. Little does Neanderthal Runner know how much better his life would be with a $499.99 Garmin Fenix 3 multisport training GPS watch. Its heart-rate monitoring and recording, omnidirectional stainless steel antenna, three-axis compass, altimeter, and barometer are ideal for those long hot days on the savannah. Look out, gazelles. You are toast.

Smartphone. Another problem Neanderthal Runner had in the past was lack of service in the bush. Problem solved. Now, with the right apps, he can turn his phone into a fitness-improvement tool, although we'll first need to show him how to operate his phone and what an app is. We'll also teach him how to do social media, surf the Web, take selfies, and shoot video. He may even want to chat with his friends while he's running.

Happily, too, he can finally bid adieu to dialing into the sounds of Mother Nature when he runs. *Bo-ring.* With a phone or armband iPod he can now listen to his favorite beats. Some vintage suggestions for his playlist: "I am a paleontologist," They Might Be Giants; "Neanderthal Man," Hot Legs; "Apeman," The Kinks; and the classic "Meet the Flintstones."

Energy gels, energy bars, energy chews, energy beans. Neanderthal Runner will be amazed by these tasty sources of energy and nutrition that help get you to the finish when you're tired. No more disgusting tearing of animal flesh with his teeth to feel satisfied. But again, let's make sure he doesn't eat the packaging. The good stuff, tell him, is *inside.*

Energy drinks. Same as for energy snacks, he'll be blown away by the astounding selection of brands and flavors. Who needs regular water when you can drink flavored water and, for that matter, caffeinated fruit punch, strawberry, black cherry, grape, mango, tangerine, and orange sports drinks? Be wary of lemon lime, however. In his primitive Homo sapiens stage of development he may confuse the contents of this drink with the golden liquid that he himself produces. Thinking that this is what twenty-first-century runners like, he may see an empty bottle, fill it with his own juices, and hand it to you as a gift. Despite the fact that he is visiting from a million years ago, and you most ardently wish to make him feel at home in this century, it is acceptable to politely decline his offer.

BUT WHERE WOULD HE RUN?

THEME RACE SUGGESTIONS FOR NEANDERTHALS AND OTHERS

Now that Neanderthal Runner is groomed, outfitted, and ready to rock, where can he go? What races should he attend?

Fortunately, the running world has got his (now-shaven) back. While even Google did not turn up any prehistoric caveman or cavewoman races, there are any number of fun, goofy, imaginative theme races and events that Neanderthal Runner would relish the chance to participate in.

One appeal of theme races is that people can do things they have never done before, or haven't done since childhood, or would never dream of doing under ordinary circumstances. So it is with the **Dirty Girl Mud Run** (GoDirtyGirl.com), where runners can flop in mud, crawl in mud, climb obstacles and land in mud, rub mud on their faces, and pour it over their heads. Neanderthal Runner would dig all of this, but the Dirty Girl series is for girls and women only, so he'd have to find another mud hole to play in or perhaps he'd rather get drenched in paint instead.

The Color Run (TheColorRun.com) bills itself as the original paint race, the world's first color 5K. Original or not, the idea behind it—tossing powdered forms of paint up in the air and at your friends and getting as painty as the dirty girls get muddy—has caught on everywhere, with color and glow runs occurring all over the map. The Neanderthal Runner could arrive in white and end up looking like a human rainbow. He might like that.

We are not sure, however, how he would react to the **5K Zombie Run** (ZombieRun.com). Its website explains that "you are not running against a clock—you're running from brain-hungry, virus-spreading, bloody zombies." Neanderthal Runner has just traveled a million years in time; now he's got to run an obstacle course while trying to avoid zombies who want to eat his brain? We're certain this is fun for some, but this may not be the right recreational fit for our guy.

A better choice might be to become a Neanderthal glow stick at the **Firefly Run** (TheFireFlyRun.com), which, like so many of these themed events, is a national series with races in various cities. Runners carry lights and they wear glowing headbands, glow sticks on their foreheads and necks, and blinking blue, green, and red LED light bands on their arms and legs. When all these thousands of self-lit people take off en masse, at night, the effect is—dare we say it—electric.

Though we've spent a great deal of time and effort grooming and shaving Neanderthal Runner, he might nevertheless enjoy donning a fake mustache or painting one on for the **5K Mustache Dache** (MustacheDache.com). If that's a hit, we can send him to Beverly Shores, Indiana, for the **Necktie 5K Walk & Run** (NeckTieRun.com), a Father's Day event where everyone is encouraged to wear a necktie in honor of dear old dad. On second thought, we better not because this might make him homesick for Neanderthal Mother and Neanderthal Father, who could not make the trip with him.

At **Bad Prom Run** (BadProm.com) the girls dress up in their vision of the worst high school prom dress ever or a bridesmaid outfit from hell. Guys are invited to play dress-up too, and they can wear bad tuxes or go a different route—makeup, wig, and an appallingly awful prom dress too. We'll let Neanderthal Runner make up his own mind on this one. Another sort of unfashionable fashion statement he

QUOTABLE SNOB

"Running is the most elemental sport there is. We are genetically programmed to do it. One might even say we are the free-ranging, curious, restless creatures that we are because of running."

—JOHN JEROME, author–runner

T-SHIRT APOCALYPSE: WHAT IF THE RUNNING WORLD SUDDENLY HAD NO TEES?

Imagine a scenario in which all the races described in this book and all the races everywhere stopped giving away T-shirts to runners and volunteers.

Such a bizarre, apocalyptic scenario will never occur, and we can all be grateful for this because if it did happen, look at all the questions that would need to be asked and answered.

WHERE WOULD THE SPONSORS PUT ALL THEIR LOGOS?

This is truly a dilemma. There are so many sponsor logos on the back of some race tees that it's like Lil Wayne (remember him?) posing on the cover of *Rolling Stone* without his shirt. There's not an empty space to be found anywhere. Theoretically logos could be placed on running shorts, although they are such tiny pieces of fabric and we're not sure that a major corporation coughing up millions in sponsorship dough wants to have its logo splashed across someone's buttocks. We'll keep thinking on this one.

WITHOUT A T-SHIRT, HOW COULD YOU TELL PEOPLE THAT YOU'VE RUN THE POLKA TROT 5K OR THE SEE JANE RUN HALF WITHOUT, YOU KNOW, ACTUALLY TELLING THEM?

Good question. Subtext is everything when it comes to T-shirts. A stranger will recognize you as a runner simply by the fact of your T-shirt and how fine you look in it. Lacking that, be sure your expensive Garmin is subtly visible to all and perhaps drop a random Emil Zatopek reference into the dinner-table conversation.

WOULD RUNNING ITSELF FADE AWAY AND DIE IF THERE WERE NO T-SHIRTS?

Unlikely. But some races have carved out unique identities in part because of their distinctive T-shirts. Three of them come to mind: Nebraska's Beer and Bagel Off-Road Run (its motto: "I'm a drinker with a running problem"); a California half marathon in Livermore wine country ("Run, Wine, Liv," a clever play on words); and the Run Thru Hell 5K and 8K in Hell Creek, Michigan ("I Ran Thru Hell"). "Everybody wants to say they've run through Hell and survived it," said one runner who has done it multiple times and snagged its coveted T-shirt.

might like is the **Ugly Sweater 5K Run** (TheUglySweaterRun.com). Runners parade around before Christmas in the ugliest sweaters they can make or buy.

And finally, what will surely be his favorite: the **Caliente Bare Dare 5K** (CalienteResorts.com), held annually at the Caliente Resort in Land O' Lakes, Florida, a self-described "clothing optional" resort that is really more of a "clothing off" resort. Neanderthal Runner will join others romping naked around the grounds of the resort. Released from his shoes and the other modern gadgets and conventions that have been forced upon him, he can once again return to his natural state and be free.

HOW TO TALK RUNNER

A GUIDE TO RUNNERSPEAK

Runners have their own language, their own way of saying things. This is part of their charm, part of what makes them runners.

If you work in the cubicle next to one, however, or if you're dating one or married to one or friends with one, the language barrier can be occasionally daunting. *What in the world did she just say?* Herewith a guide to runnerspeak—words and acronyms used by runners.

BAA. Boston Athletic Association. Also what a sheep says: "Baa."

BQ. Also: BQ'd. Boston qualified. This means you have run a time that meets the qualifying standards for entering the Boston Marathon. This is a true accomplishment, so you should go out and treat yourself to some BBQ.

BRS. Blue Ribbon Sports, the original name of the company that became Nike. Will win you points if you drop it into a conversation in Eugene, but will cost you dearly if you do the same in Seattle (home of Brooks) or Boston (New Balance).

Carbo-load. Once upon a time, this was an esoteric term for loading up on pasta before a big race. Not anymore; it's part of mainstream vocabulary now. When Kevin Costner in *McFarland USA* says that

One thing a runner should never do is tell someone that a marathon is 26 miles. It is most decidedly *not* 26 miles; it is 26.2 miles. Those 385 yards mean *everything*.

the Hispanic kids he is coaching in cross-country are "carbo-loading rice and beans all day," it's a sure bet the audience understood what he was saying.

DFL. Dead F**king Last. Or Dead Freaking Last, for those who dislike asterisks. Many popular running acronyms begin with D, such as: DNF: Did Not Finish. DNS: Did Not Start. DNQ: Did Not Qualify.

ER. Endurance Running. Too much ER can sometimes send runners to the ER.

FKT. Fastest Known Time. A term popularized by ultrarunners and extreme athletes to measure the hours and days it takes them to climb high peaks and cross wide deserts. Some difficult ascents and crossings have never been done before so FKT is how they measure it. An RT—round-trip—is up and down a mountain. And if you run to the top of an obscure mountain in record time, you can use arguably the greatest acronym ever invented: FKT UP.

Kilometer. No one in America actually knows how far a kilometer is. A thousand meters? Okay, got it. Tell a nonrunner you're running a 5K next week, and he or she will nod blankly and say, "Remind me again. How far is that?"

LSD. Long Slow Distance, a marathon training technique commonly associated with author–runner Joe Henderson. Not to be confused with LSD the drug, although it is true that some runners do experience hallucinogenic states while making LSD runs over extreme distances.

PF. Plantar Fasciitis. A foot ailment suffered by runners. Other fun acronyms are PFPS—patellofemoral pain syndrome, aka runner's knee—and ITBS—illiotibial band syndrome, which is related to hip pain. Minor pains can be helped by what Rachel Toor calls "Vitamin I"—ibuprofen.

QUOTABLE SNOB

Asked once if he ever felt like taking a day off from his daily training regimen to rest and heal, the great Japanese marathoner Toshihiko Seko replied, "Of course. All the time."

PR. Personal Record. Your best time ever for a given distance. Also PB, or Personal Best, which is the opposite of PW, Personal Worst.

Pronate/Supinate. Scientific tests have shown that if you use either of these words in a casual conversation with a nonrunner, her eyes will glaze over and her mind will go blank, unless she is a podiatrist, in which case she may be fascinated. If pronate and supinate do turn out to be conversation starters for you, talk next about the value of maintaining the appropriate "stride length." Things will really start buzzing between the two of you then.

Rabbit. Other terms for it are *pacemaker* or *pace-setter,* a person who goes out fast to set the early pace in a race to push the other runners to faster times. The best cinematic use of the term *rabbit*, or more properly *wabbit*, came in Bill Murray's timeless existential epic, *Meatballs*, in which he urges a young boy named Rudy to make like a rabbit and bound through the woods to win a race. Murray calls him "Wootie the Wabbit" and yells: "Run, you wascal wabbit, run!" Spoiler alert: Wootie wins.

Splits. Not what a ballet dancer does, but your time for a segment or segments of a race. A "negative split" is when your time in the second half of a race is faster than in the first half. The word *negative* is used even though you are running faster than before, which, generally speaking, is a positive.

Sub. Not to be confused with the sandwich, *sub* is a prefix often used by runners. As in: "sub-four," a mile run under 4 minutes, or "sub-3 hours," a coveted time for a marathon.

VO2. Short for "VO2 max," which is a measure of an athlete's cardiovascular fitness, the maximum amount of oxygen he or she can use during exercise. Runners being as cool as a Wynton Marsalis trumpet solo, they also use shorthand when referring to their heart rate; it's HR. Maximum heart rate when working out: HRMax.

WR. World Record. Another shorthand term used mainly by elite runners. Drop a WR on your pals while chatting during your next 5K fun run and impress all.

RUNNING SNOB QUIZ #5

RUNNING MOVIES

"My momma always said, 'Life was like a box of chocolates. You never know what you're gonna get.'"

If you do not know what movie that comes from, and whose momma said it, you may struggle with this chapter's quiz on running movies. But how you do on the quiz is of course no reflection on your intelligence, because, as we all know, "Stupid is as stupid does." Answers follow the quiz.

1. Louis Zamperini ran the 5,000 meters for the United States in the 1936 Berlin Olympic Games and later endured incredible hardship during World War II in a Japanese POW camp. His story is told in a beautiful film directed by Angelina Jolie based on the book by Lauren Hillenbrand. Name the title of the movie and book.
   a. *Unforgiven*
   b. *Unbreakable*
   c. *Unbroken*
   d. *Undeniable*

2. In *Without Limits*, the biopic of Steve Prefontaine directed by *Chinatown's* Robert Towne and cowritten by Kenny Moore, Pre receives free shoes that he runs in and gives away to girls. What shoe company supplied these shoes?
   a. Brooks
   b. adidas
   c. Nike
   d. New Balance

3. The title character of *Forrest Gump* also receives a gift of running shoes from his beloved girlfriend Jenny. What shoes did she give him, which he then used to run across America in the movie?
   a. Brooks
   b. adidas
   c. Nike
   d. New Balance

4. Arnold Schwarzenegger plays the lead in 1987's *The Running Man*, a futuristic thriller based on a Stephen King novel in which the contestants in a television program must survive a series of life-or-death violent attacks. These are all lines of dialog from Schwarzenegger movies. Which one came from *Running Man*?

  a. "Hasta la vista, baby."

  b. "Remember. I can break your neck like a chicken."

  c. "No matter what anyone tells you, Bane, it really is the size of your gun that counts."

  d. "Thank you for the cookies. I look forward to tossing them."

5. Let's do that again. The young Bill Murray starred as a camp counselor in *Meatballs*, a goofball teen comedy about a summer camp. He and a young boy go on morning runs together, and the boy relies on this training to win the movie's climactic cross-country race. All four of these lines are from Bill Murray movies. Which one did Murray say in *Meatballs*?

  a. "I make it a rule never to get involved with possessed people."

  b. "I killed myself so many times I don't even exist anymore."

  c. "Chicks dig me, because I rarely wear underwear and when I do it's usually something unusual."

  d. "Roxanne, I have what doctors call 'very active glands.' You're the first person I've told, my folks don't even know."

6. *The Loneliness of the Long Distance Runner* is a 1962 English film based on the influential short story of the same name by Alan Sillitoe, who wrote the script. Its finale also ends with a race—a cross-country race between the rebellious young anti-hero (played by Tom Courtenay) and a prep school rival. How does the race end?

  a. Courtenay wins easily.

  b. Courtenay trips and falls dramatically, but gets up to nip the prep school boy in a close finish.

c. Courtenay stops to let the preppie beat him.

d. Courtenay wins by cheating, tripping the boy when no one is looking.

7. A superb and heartbreaking Australian war movie, *Gallipoli*, stars the young Mel Gibson as a speedy runner who delivers messages between battle commanders on the front lines much as runners have done since the time of Pheidippides and before. Gallipoli was an actual battle in what war?

a. World War II

b. Spanish Civil War

c. World War I

d. Boer War

8. *Chariots of Fire*, based on the stories of British sprint champions Eric Liddell and Harold Abrahams at the 1924 Olympics, won four Oscars, including best picture and best music and original score. Its opening and closing shots of the boys running on the beach may be the most parodied scene in movie history. Name the composer who wrote the theme music.

a. John Williams

b. Giorgio Moroder

c. Ennio Morricone

d. Vangelis

9. In *McFarland USA* Kevin Costner plays a coach who forms a cross-country team at a poor, largely Hispanic high school in California. Although the team (spoiler alert) goes on to win the state championship, no one thinks this is a good idea at first, including the school principal. He opposes it, telling Costner, "Cross-country? That's a private school sport. They don't breathe the same air we do." What does Costner say in response?

a. "Rich, poor. Doesn't matter. Everybody runs."

b. "They breathe the same air."

c. "Yeah, but we can learn to breathe it too."

d. "That's my job. I'm the coach. They'll learn."

10. *The Robber* is a dark, art house–style German film about a violent criminal who is a long- distance runner. Based on a true story, the movie shows the main character winning a big city marathon in Austria. When he's not running marathons, what does he rob?

a. Banks

b. Commuter trains

c. Convenience stores

d. Casinos

Answers: 1. c; 2. b; 3. c; 4. b; 5. d; 6. c; 7. c; 8. d; 9. b; 10. a

CHAPTER SIX

Adventures in Running

When you start out as a runner, and even after you've become quite experienced, you are always testing your limits. How far can you go? How fast? For how long? As you get stronger and more confident, a crazy thing happens: You start crashing through those limits and establishing new limits for yourself, going well beyond what you ever thought you could do. This is one of the great adventures of running—how you keep discarding limits like old shoes and acquiring new ones. In this chapter we push through the limits and explore some of running's greatest challenges: ultramarathons, barefoot running, triathlons, team relays, and more.

ULTRAMARATHON FAQS

The word *ultra*, according to the Oxford dictionary, means "extreme," which, we must say, is an outrageous and inflammatory tag to hang on ultramarathoners and ultrarunners. These men and women are not extreme; they merely run incredibly long distances for hours and sometimes days in intense heat and cold over mountains and deserts that most people would never dream of crossing unless they were in the window seat of a passenger jet.

To promote better understanding and to refute this baseless charge of extremism, here are answers to some commonly asked questions about ultrarunners and what they do.

Q: Let's start at the start. What is an ultramarathon?

A: Technically, an ultra, as the cognoscenti refer to it, is any footrace beyond 26.2 miles, the standard marathon distance. Ultras can be 50K (31 miles), 50 miles, 100K (62 miles), 100 miles (a "Century"), 250K (155 miles)—or anything between those distances and sometimes greater than them too.

Q: Where are the races held?

A: Anywhere and everywhere. In the United States, around the world, on all the continents. An around-the-planet run could be classified

as an ultra and if such a thing is ever organized, there will be a line of ultrarunners waiting to sign up for it.

Q: How long does it take to complete an ultra?

A: Depends on the ultra. It can take a day, several days, a week. They're like that old Lionel Richie song; they go all night long, and in the frigid cold and blistering heat too.

Q: What sort of people do ultramarathons?

A: A know-nothing cynic might answer, "Extreme masochists." But this is not fair and not right. Ultrarunners are just like everyone else, only different. "One group of people think I'm crazy, [that] there's something wrong upstairs," Irish ultrarunner Dave O'Brien explained in the documentary *Desert Runners*, while preparing for a 250K race in Chile. "Another group of people think, 'Good for you.'"

Q: Why do they do it?

A: The personal challenge, mainly. In every race there are always people who are out to win—be first man, first woman, grab the gold in their age group. This is true in ultramarathons too. But the bulk of people are competing against themselves. Pushing through personal barriers to prove they can do it, that sort of thing. The unconventional aspects also appeal to them; they're doing something that the general population, including many runners, look at with horror and would never attempt. And they often must travel to faraway places to run them, which adds to the mystique.

Q: Is it acceptable to walk as well as run?

A: Yes. Ultramarathoners run, walk, walk fast, walk slow, shuffle, crawl, slide down cliffs, climb over rocks, slip on ice patches, swoon, keel over, get up, roll, tumble, and stagger but always, they hope, keep going. If you're not comfortable with the idea of subjecting yourself to mind-exploding, body-annihilating levels of pain, it's probably not the sport for you.

Q: Do ultrarunners experience the legendary "runner's high" we hear so much about?

A: Some do. You run so far for so long that it can develop into an out-of-body experience. His body breaking down and his mind undergoing hallucinations in the latter stages of the Lake Saroma 100K in Japan, Haruki Murakami described the phenomenon in these words: "First there came the action of running, and accompanying it there was this entity known as me. I'm me, and at the same time not me." The positive thing about this is that if your mind and body detach from each other, you still only have to pay for one registration.

Q: Who are some famous ultrarunners?

A: Kilian Jornet Burgada is amazing. He has won all the big ultras and has run up and down the Matterhorn and Denali as well as other peaks. Rob Krar ran from the South Rim of the Grand Canyon to the North Rim and back again, about 42 miles in over six hours. Dean Karnazes endured 250K races across four different deserts on four different continents—the Atacama in Chile, the Gobi in China, the Sahara, and Antarctica—all in the same year, the first person to do this. Women do ultras too, and they're good at them. Ann Trason has won the women's division of the Western States 100, Leadville Trail 100, and many other prestigious ultras multiple times.

SNOB ASIDE

One could make a strong case that Pheidippides was an early ultrarunner. Although today we associate him mainly with the marathon, because he covered about that many miles in his most famous run, he also supposedly ran a much longer distance to ask for Sparta's help in the Athenian battle against the invading Persians. That distance has been estimated to be around 152 miles. The Sparthathlon is an ultrarace held in Greece every year to commemorate his feat; it begins in Athens, ends in Sparta, and covers 152 miles, or 246K.

Q: When you run an ultra, do you get a T-shirt and medal like with other races?

A: Sure you do. You can also get heatstroke, your blood pressure can rise to life-threatening levels, you can fall and break an ankle or wrist, you can get so dehydrated they have to set you up with an IV to replenish your bodily fluids, you can experience heart arrhythmia, you can get overexposed to the sun and heat and pass out, you can come down with high-altitude pulmonary edema, and you can punish every joint and muscle in your body to such a degree that you may not be able to walk without pain for days or weeks. On the plus side, they throw all this other stuff in for free.

Q: Wow. Sounds like my kind of race. Can you list some ultraraces where I can experience this kind of fun?

A: Glad you asked. Our next section lists some of the best.

THE SNOB 10

OUTSTANDING ULTRAS
FROM 50 MILES AND UP

"What we do," says Kilian Jornet Burgada, widely regarded as the world's best ultrarunner and trail runner, "isn't serious."

Perhaps not, when compared to global issues of war and peace. But one thing is certain: If you're thinking about entering an ultra, you better approach it *seriously*. It's a mental and physical test of the first degree. Here are ten outstanding ultras from 50 miles and up.

JFK 50 MILE

The JFK 50 began in the spring of 1963 after President John F. Kennedy issued his famous call for Americans to exercise more and get into better shape. After his death many of the races and exercise events that were inspired by him fell away. But not the JFK 50. The next year it changed its name—from the JFK 50 Mile Challenge to the JFK 50 Mile Memorial—and in the decades since it has become a star of the East Coast ultracircuit. Start inland in Maryland in Boonsboro, follow the Appalachian Trail, and finish strong in Williamsport on the Potomac River. Many of the participants are US military. JFK50Mile.org

ICE AGE TRAIL 50

Like many a grand and noble venture, the origins of the Ice Age Trail 50 can be traced back to a pub. This particular pub was one of Milwaukee's finest, and it was where ultrarunner Tom Ulik and Glenn Wargolet of the Badgerland Striders running club held a serious evening of drinking, thinking, and talking. At the time there was no 50-mile race in Wisconsin or anywhere else in the Midwest—a deficiency the two men sorely wished to remedy. And so they did. Ulik had the perfect spot for it—the Southern Kettle Moraine Forest, an ancient enchanted land of "kettles" or small glacially formed lakes, hills, and prairies—and this is where the Ice Age kicks off every May. And, in the spirit of its founding, one or two cold beers are consumed after. IceAgeTrail50.com

TABLE ROCK ULTRA

Table Rock is one of the most striking sights along the Blue Ridge Parkway in the green mountains of North Carolina. "There are not a lot of mountains shaped like that around here," says Brandon Thrower, who lives on the Blue Ridge. "From some angles it looks like a thumb sticking out of the sky." Thrower is co-race director of the Table Rock 50K and 50-Mile races that climb to the 4,000-foot summit of that thumb in the sky. There, runners can catch their breath and see across the Linville Gorge Wilderness. But don't tarry long; there's another 25 miles to go before the finish in Steele Creek Park. TableRockUltras.com

BULLDOG 50K

The home of the Bulldog 25K and 50K is Malibu Creek State Park. Since Malibu is in the title, this might suggest carefree romps along the white sand beaches of the Pacific Coast Highway, near the luxurious beachside bungalows of Barbra Streisand and other Hollywood celebs. Not a chance. Malibu Creek State Park covers wide swatches of the Santa Monica Mountains, which are steep, gnarly, littered with poison oak, and home to many an angry rattlesnake. Stay away from the critters and don't forget to hydrate, because race day is normally as hot as Streisand's record sales used to be. TrailRunEvents.com

WESTERN STATES 100

The granddaddy of them all. The world's oldest 100-mile trail race, and some would say still the best. Beginning in the 1950s they held a trail ride that went from Lake Tahoe to Auburn in the Sierra Nevada mountains. The ride, known as the Western States Trail Ride or Tevis Cup, challenged horses and their mounts to travel the 100 miles in a single day, following the original trails used by the gold miners and pioneers of the 1850s. The trails climbed more than 18,000 feet and dropped another 23,000 before ending in Auburn in the foothills.

Then, in 1974, a man named Gordon Ainsleigh decided to do something different—very, very different. Having ridden the Tevis Cup, he wondered if he could do it all, in a single day, *on foot*. This seemingly crackpot idea contained the seeds of genius. That first run Ainsleigh finished in 23 hours and 42 minutes, proving that a man on foot could match a horse and rider and get there in less than a day. The ultra-running ancestors of Ainsleigh (he's still around, sporting a nice silver beard perfect for an elder statesman) migrate to the Western States every year, covering ground where only horses used to go. Wser.org

LEADVILLE TRAIL 100

The wooden sign on the outskirts of town says, "Welcome to historic Leadville. On top of it all." Above 10,000 feet elevation in the Rockies, Leadville does indeed seem to be on top of it all, a one-time mining town that has reinvented itself as one of the modern capitals of ultra–trail running. The 100 begins in Leadville at night, with everyone taking off in headlamps, and later ends in the same place, on Main Street. Runners run, walk, and stagger through pine forests, across creeks, up and over the 12,600-foot Hope Pass, all around trails and big mountains topped by glacial snow. LeadvilleRaceSeries.com

QUOTABLE SNOB

"There was no easy part. I died a couple of times."

—MIKE AISH, after finishing second at Leadville, expressing the thoughts of everyone who has competed in the Colorado 100-miler and indeed, in ultras everywhere.

THE HARDROCK 100

The Hardrock 100-Mile Endurance Run is another heavy-duty trail run across the Colorado Rockies, beginning and ending in Silverton. Finishers do not run across a finish line as in the customary fashion;

instead, they kiss a boulder with a picture of a ram's head on it. This signifies the race is over for them. Underneath the ram's picture are the words "Wild & Tough," which you surely can claim to be if you smooch that ram. The boulder is actually a piece of debris that was pulled from a mine in Silverton, which, like Leadville, is a former mining town that retains its old Wild West flavor. Hardrock100.com

BADWATER 135

Virtually every extreme ultramarathon, the most extreme ones in any case, claims to be the "world's toughest footrace." The Badwater 135-miler may actually deserve the title. It starts in Death Valley, the lowest elevation in North America at 280 feet below sea level. Death Valley did not receive its name without cause; it is a barren, Godforsaken landscape that regularly registers some of the hottest temperatures on Earth. The Badwater ends in the mountains of the Sierra Nevada, at the Whitney Portal about 8,300 feet above sea level. Runners cross three mountain ranges and climb a total of 14,600 vertical feet and descend about 6,100. The winners take about a day to finish; the stragglers start coming in around forty hours. Everyone who finishes receives a silver belt buckle with a skull on it, and deserves it. Badwater.com

SNOB ADVICE

Physical preparation—getting fit, training hard, getting your gear right—is vital for ultra success. So is learning to become mentally strong. There is, after all, no real reason to run 50 miles except for your own desire and determination, which is reason enough. And this is what will ultimately carry you through the pain and hardship. "It hurts up to a point," ultrarunner Ann Trason observed, "and then it doesn't get any worse."

COMRADES MARATHON

Alberto Salazar describes Comrades as "part spectacle, part national holiday, part sporting event, part survival trek." Salazar won this "marathon"—it's really an ultra, being 90K or about 56 miles, from Pietermaritzburg to Durban, South Africa—at the end of his illustrious career. It was in fact his last win before retiring from competition, and the five-hour-plus endurance test forced him to call on every bit of strength he had. The only reason he made it, he said later, "was that I had taken my ego and will completely out of the equation and put the race in God's hands." Begun after World War I in 1921, Comrades honors the millions who died in that awful bloody conflict as well as those who fought and survived. Comrades.com

ULTRA TRAIL MONT BLANC

Straddling the borders of France, Switzerland, and Italy, Mont Blanc is one of the world's most beautiful and dangerous peaks. Two French mountaineers, Jacques Balmat and Michel Paccard, climbed it first in 1786. Many more have followed, while others have gotten caught in brutal snowstorms or suffered other misfortunes and died in the attempt. The Ultra Trail Mont Blanc, known as UTMB in the ultra world, crosses high mountain passes, valleys, and glaciers, all within sight of that majestic snow-topped peak, the tallest in the Alps. The UTMB is a kind of European tour all by itself. It begins in Italy and, after 105 miles, finishes with a flourish in the glorious French skiing village of Chamonix. UltraTrailMB.com

RUN LIKE THE KENYANS

A 7-STEP DISTANCE-RUNNING TRAINING GUIDE

For years the leading coaches, trainers, and runners of the West have been making pilgrimages to Kenya's Rift Valley to discover why the Kenyans—as well as their neighbors in Ethiopia—have been grabbing so many titles and winning so much money on the global professional racing circuit. There are many theories as to why this is.

Fortunately the Snob has sifted through all these theories and boiled them down into this easy seven-step training program, thus saving you the time, trouble, and expense of going to Africa yourself to learn these secrets. Follow this step-by-step guide and you too can run like those remarkable Kenyans.

STEP ONE: RUN EVERY DAY AT 6 IN THE MORNING, EVEN IF IT'S DARK OUTSIDE.

Adharanand Finn, a British writer and runner who moved to Kenya to build his endurance and run a marathon, found that that's what everybody does. They don't think about it, they just do it. They get up, they run. One reason is because it gets so bloody hot during the day and they can beat the heat by going early. When they do two-a-days, their second run is in the cool of the evening.

STEP TWO: RUN ONLY ON GRASS OR DIRT.

Except when they travel to big cities to run and win prestigious marathons, the Kenyans prefer to stay away from asphalt or concrete when they train. This is, of course, more easily done on the high plains of Africa where lions still prowl around. Sometimes lions actually wander into races in progress, forcing officials to use helicopters to shoo them away so they do not attack and, presumably, eat any of the runners or spectators. This may be another, less widely publicized reason for Kenyan success: They learn at an early age to run faster than lions.

STEP 3: RUN IN A GROUP.

The Kenyans avoid some of the motivational struggles that individuals face because they generally train in groups, not alone. "It can feel as though the group is running, not you, as if the movement around you has picked you up and is carrying you along," writes Finn, who nevertheless fails to mention in his analysis the just-noted LFF (Lion Fear Factor). Kenyans may run all bunched up to protect themselves against lions and also, possibly, snakes. Snakes grow very large in the Rift Valley and are known to hide in termite mounds that form inside homes when the residents leave for a while. When the residents return, the snakes emerge.

SNOB ASIDE

The 2016 London Marathon had a novel twist. Tim Peake, a British astronaut, ran the race on a treadmill from the International Space Station simultaneous with the marathon taking place on Earth. He watched a video of the course streets in real-time and finished in 3 hours, 35 minutes, 21 seconds, the second person to run a marathon in space. Otherwise London went according to form; two Kenyans, Eliud Kipchoge and Jemima Sumgong, won the men's and women's races, respectively.

STEP 4: EAT *UGALI* DAILY.

The staple of life in Kenya, for runners and everyone else, is *ugali*, a thick cornbread-like food made from corn flour and water. It looks like oatmeal or mashed potatoes when you're making it, and it fills you up even more than a Denny's Grand Slam. Kenyans essentially carbo-load every day, dipping *ugali* into stews and using it much the same as we use bread.

STEP 5: GET LOTS AND LOTS OF MASSAGE THERAPY.

This is a good one. The Kenyans believe strongly in the value of massage as a way to limber up their muscles, relieve aches and tension, and stimulate circulation throughout the body. They also believe massage helps them get back to training and competing more quickly after an injury. Quite a few Kenyans become so expert in massage therapy that after retiring from competition, they turn to it as a career.

STEP 6: MOVE TO THE MOUNTAINS.

Most of the elite Kenyan runners are members of the Kalenjin Tribe, living and training at mountainous elevations above 5,000 feet. Although not moving to Africa, many elite American runners have adopted this strategy, moving to mountain towns such as Boulder, Flagstaff, and Mammoth Lakes to train at high elevation. Here's a potential business opportunity for runners in these towns: open up an *ugali* bakery.

STEP 7: RUN OR WALK EVERYWHERE YOU GO— IN BARE FEET.

Every elite Kenyan runner—*every one!*—grew up in poor, rural surroundings, walking and running everywhere they went. They ran to and from school, and they ran out to the fields to tend the goats and cattle. And they did all this in their bare feet, without benefit of lucrative shoe endorsement contracts. Running without shoes, especially when young, is a key ingredient in the Kenyan formula for success, and one that everyone in serious pursuit of distance-running marathon glory should not neglect. On your next run, leave your shoes at home. Just watch out for broken glass on the street.

BAREFOOT RUNNERS OF FACT AND LEGEND

THE BAREFOOT RUNNER OF LOS ANGELES, AND MORE

For its adherents, barefoot running is the essence of what running is and ideally should be. Going without shoes, they feel, makes them less prone to injury and enhances their enjoyment of the sport. One thing is for sure: If you see someone running without shoes, it turns your head. It's a conversation starter.

As odd as it may seem to most people, including most runners, barefoot running has a long and proud heritage. Here are a few stories about barefoot runners, in legend and fact.

The Kalahari Bushmen. This small African tribe of aboriginals, in existence for hundreds of years but now sadly in danger of extinction, lives in the remote Kalahari Desert, where they hunt as they

have for generations—on foot, by running down their prey. Years ago the BBC series *Planet Earth*, narrated by David Attenborough, followed the Kalahari on "a persistence hunt" for a kudu bull. Persistence is the perfect word for it because that is what the tribesmen must show—a steady, undeniable, relentless persistence in a day-long hunt that crosses tens of miles across the African bush.

The lead Kalahari hunter earns this distinction by being the fastest and strongest endurance runner in the tribe. Although a few of the hunters wear ragged sports-style shoes, others go barefoot the way their fathers and grandfathers did. By day's end, unable to outrun the implacable men on its trail, the kudu is utterly exhausted and beaten, so tired it can no longer run or even stand fully. It has collapsed to two legs when the chief hunter plunges his spear into its side.

The Tarahumara Indians. In Christopher McDougall's classic *Born to Run*, he investigates the mysterious Tarahumara Indians of Mexico, whom he describes as "a near mystical tribe of Stone Age superathletes." They run mostly barefoot and over long, long distances. One champion brave reportedly ran 435 miles continuously, day and night, stopping only for short breaks. Others run for dozens of miles at a time, finally exhausting the deer they are chasing, much like the Kalahari and the kudu.

A climb to the top of a mountain in their home in the Barrancas del Cobre—Copper Canyon—can take ten hours by mule, but a fast Tarahumara can do the same trip in less than two hours. There is a catch, however. Their extraordinary powers of speed and stamina are due, it is said, to a secret elixir of which only they know the recipe.

Abebe Bikila. The most magical moment in competitive barefoot running history occurred in 1960 when Bikila, a private in the Ethiopian military, ran through the cobblestone streets of Rome at night to win the gold medal in the Olympic marathon, the first East African to do so. The shoes issued by the Ethiopian team did not fit him, so he carried on without them, setting a world record of 2 hours, 12 minutes, 2 seconds and winning the hearts of millions for the charming audaciousness of what he had done. He often trained without shoes and ran barefoot as a boy.

QUOTABLE SNOB

"I can still remember quite vividly a time when as a child I ran barefoot along damp firm sand by the seashore. It was an intense moment of discovery of a source of power and beauty that one previously hardly dreamt existed."

—ROGER BANNISTER, the first to break four minutes for the mile

Zola Budd. Budd was a gifted, yet star-crossed teenage barefoot runner who unfortunately got cast as a villain in one of the most heartbreaking moments in Olympic Games history, at least for US track. It occurred in 1984 in Los Angeles in the finals of the women's 3,000 meters. The pre-race favorite was the brilliant Mary Decker Slaney, a former teen phenom herself who was Prefontaine-like in her domination of American distance running, holding every national record from the 800 meters to the 10,000 meters. Entering the Olympics, she was the reigning world champion in the 3,000 meters and 10,000 meters.

Then disaster struck. Budd, a South African who was competing for Great Britain in the Games and who was inexperienced in international competition, was leading the race in a tight group of four runners with Decker close behind her in second. Decker tripped on the back of Budd's foot and fell to the infield grabbing her leg in pain. She writhed on the grass, her tears in part caused by the knowledge that she was out of the race and her Olympic dreams were over.

Budd continued on and maintained the lead for a short time, but fell off the pace and finished seventh as the boos cascaded down on her from the partisan American crowd. The bitter Decker Slaney blamed Budd for causing the incident, and the South African was disqualified and later reinstated by the judges. The two runners met and reconciled some time later, although the hurt surely still lingers for them both.

The Barefoot Runner of Los Angeles. On a lighter note, there is the Barefoot Runner of Los Angeles, who is bearded and shaggy, somewhat like that famous if mysterious barefoot runner of the Pacific Northwest, Sasquatch. But unlike Sasquatch, the Barefoot Runner of Los Angeles actually does exist. His name is Ken Bob Saxton, and Chris McDougall has called him "the great bearded sage" of barefoot running in this country. In one interview Saxton explained that he feels bad for shoe-clad runners because "they've lost touch, literally, with the ground. You can tell a barefoot runner by the smile on his face."

He loves the freedom that running barefoot gives him, saying, "It feels good to feel the breeze blow across the tops of my feet." Barefoot runners are a proudly individualistic bunch, but they relish getting together with like-minded people same as everyone else. Those in quest of solidarity should try Saxon's group, the Barefoot Runners Society (BarefootRunning.com).

HOW ABOUT TRYING A TRI?

6 THINGS TO KEEP IN MIND BEFORE YOU SWIM, BIKE, AND RUN A TRIATHLON

As they push the boundaries of personal development and fitness, many runners contemplate doing a triathlon. We think triathlons are marvelous events, and we heartily encourage giving it a go, as the Brits might say.

It is, however, not a thing you should rush into willy-nilly. Here are six things to keep in mind if you are thinking about trying a tri.

1. A TRIATHLON IS AN ENDURANCE EVENT THAT COMBINES SWIMMING, BICYCLING, *AND* RUNNING.

Obvious, right? Well, yes it is. But one must never lose sight of the fact that each of these disciplines has its own set of muscles and skills, and that each requires training to develop. And that requires time, long hours of it, not to mention specialized equipment such as a bicycle. That you will need to spend hundreds and perhaps thousands for a triathlon or road bike will come as a shock to no one except, perhaps, certain runners who are accustomed to paying virtually nothing (after their shoes) to do their sport. Then there is the little business of finding a pool to train in.

These challenges are hardly insurmountable, of course, and lots of runners move into triathlons with nary a hitch. One way to ease the transition is to start out with what is called "a sprint triathlon"—a somewhat less-demanding version of the event (the terms are all relative because every triathlon is demanding in its way) that might call for a 1,500-meter swim, 25-mile bicycle leg, and a 10K, or shorter legs for all three.

2. IF YOU DO NOT KNOW HOW TO SWIM, OR DON'T LIKE TO SWIM, YOU DON'T HAVE TO SWIM.

Swimming is the most intimidating aspect of participating in a triathlon. Many are not confident of their swimming abilities or simply do not know how. Because of this at least one triathlon we know has substituted the swimming leg with a kayak leg—kayak, bike, run. Of course, if the kayak tips over and you fall out, you're still going to get wet. Other events may require only a ceremonial dip in the water to satisfy the swimming requirement.

Duathlons eliminate swimming altogether and combine cycling with running. Some of them sandwich the cycling leg between two legs of running at the start and the end, the idea being to replicate the classic three-stage nature of a triathlon.

SNOB ADVICE

If you've never swum a mile in open water before, you may privately wonder if you can even do it. So the first time you enter a race you tend to hold back and guard your reserves to make sure that you can, indeed, finish the thing. Once you do it successfully, you will have more confidence the next time out and be better able to judge how fast and hard you need to exert yourself at any point in the race. Experience is a great teacher, in distance swimming as in running.

3. THE SWIMMING TAKES PLACE IN OPEN WATER.

To make matters more challenging for those who lack confidence in their swimming, the swimming legs of virtually all triathlons are held in open water, be it a lake or bay or ocean. Swimming in open water is a far different beast than swimming in a pool. One must cope with waves, rolling swells, wind, the uneasy and disorienting feeling of being far away from land, and the cold.

Some inland lake events, and even some coastal events in southern regions, are in warm water. And if the water isn't exactly warm, it's at least manageable. Which is not the case with Escape from Alcatraz, the famous San Francisco tri that begins on Alcatraz Island, the site of the former maximum security federal prison that once held the likes of Al Capone and Machine Gun Kelly. The reason they held the baddest of the bad guys there was that even if one of them broke out of prison, where would they go? San Francisco Bay was too cold, too rough, and too treacherous to swim.

The Escape starts with a 1.5-mile swim from Alcatraz to Aquatic Park. The next two legs—an 18-mile bike ride around San Francisco's hills followed by an 8-mile footrace—are almost a pleasure after that miserable, bone-chilling yet strangely exhilarating (after you finish) swim.

4. THERE CAN BE SHARKS IN THE WATER.

Whether you are swimming in a bathtub-warm lake or a frigid bay, it can be disorienting to be out in open water with no lane lines or stripes at the bottom of the pool to guide you. Best to stick as close as you can to the pack of swimmers in the race, although sometimes an unwelcome guest can crash the party.

Yes, there have been shark sightings in San Francisco Bay and other saltwater triathlons, and in one scary case in Corona del Mar off the

southern California coast, a shark bit a woman triathlete. But it's extremely rare, and the threat is frankly minimal. Nonetheless we do not recommend watching *The Shallows* or *Jaws* as a way to relax the night before a saltwater triathlon.

5. SAME AS IN RUNNING, THERE ARE HILLS, ONLY BIGGER.

The Legend 100 in Lawrence, Kansas, is known for attracting big-name international triathletes with world championship cred—Great Britain's Chrissie Wellington, Aussie Craig Alexander, and South Africa's Simon Lessing, to name but three. One reason they come all that way is because the course is unusually flat and they can record fast times. The 100 consists of 2 miles of lake swimming, 80 miles of biking, and 18 miles of running.

Many triathlons take a different tack and emphatically embrace the hills, particularly on the bicycle leg. For instance, the 70-mile Savage-Man Triathlon in the Allegheny Mountains of western Maryland starts with a 1.2-mile swim in Deep Creek Lake, after which contestants go on a 56-mile ride highlighted—or lowlighted, one might say, depending on how much pain you're in when you're doing it—by a 2,000-foot elevation gain up Big Savage Mountain and across the Eastern Continental Divide. To finish things off (and many of the competitors as well, one would think), a half marathon follows.

6. SOMETIMES, AFTER ALL THAT SWIMMING AND BIKING, YOU MUST RUN . . . *A MARATHON*.

The marathon is the ultimate achievement in distance running, a lifetime accomplishment for some, the stuff of dreams and glory. But in the Hawaii Ironman it is merely one of three parts, the climactic final act in an intense three-act drama. The Ironman was the original triathlon to end with a marathon, and it's still the big daddy of the sport. It began in the late 1970s when Judy and John Collins, a Navy couple who were stationed in Honolulu, came up with the audacious idea of combining three of Hawaii's toughest endurance events—the 2.4-mile Wakiki Roughwater Swim, the 112-mile Around Oahu Bike Race, and the Honolulu Marathon—into one. For the first race the Collinses passed out flyers to entice a few brave souls to enter, saying that if they pulled off the seemingly impossible feat of finishing all three legs, they could "brag for the rest of your life."

The Ironman is now in Kona, on the big island of Hawaii, the site of the Ironman world championships. There are Ironman competitions around the world, as well as scads of other similarly grueling triathlons that also require contestants to swim 2.4 miles in open water, race 112 miles on a bike, and top it all off with a jaunt of 26.2 miles. If you finish an Ironman or the equivalent, you do indeed deserve to do some serious bragging. Plus, since you're on the beach in Hawaii, you might as well hang around a while and do some serious drinking, eating, and relaxing too.

THE TIMELESS APPEAL OF MUD, BEER, AND PARTIES

IF NOT A TRIATHLON, HOW ABOUT AN OBSTACLE COURSE RACE?

In an obstacle course event, you run, climb over walls, crawl under rope fences, slide down slides, cross bridges, jump off platforms into ponds of water, go hand over hand across climbing equipment, and help friends and sometimes complete strangers do all these things along the way.

They range in distance from 5Ks to marathons, with the number and severity of the obstacles depending on the event. Obstacle course events are excellent team building exercises, they pose a physical and mental challenge, and they're kind of a hoot too. Here are six reasons why.

1. THERE IS MUD, LOTS AND LOTS OF MUD.

One of the appeals of an obstacle course race is that it gives adults the chance to act like kids and do some crazy fun stuff, such as flop around in mud and get very, very dirty and wet. The marketing video for Tough Mudder, probably the best known of the obstacle course companies, delivers this message like mud in the eye. "There is no

fountain of youth," it says, "you can't go back in time. What there is, is mud." If your obstacle course race doesn't have mud, and plenty of it, find another.

2. THERE IS BEER, LOTS AND LOTS OF BEER.
Beer is almost as prevalent as mud. The beer comes later, of course, at the post-race party. But what else are you going to do seeing that you're dressed only in your skivvies and covered head to toe in mud? Convene a study group of Tolstoy's *Anna Karenina*? No, you're going to have a Sam Adams or a Lagunitas, and probably more than two.

3. THE OBSTACLES HAVE FUNNY NAMES.
The obstacles are fun and challenging, and their names are clever too. Birth Canal, Electroshock Therapy, Arctic Enema 2.0, and Funky Monkey are four Tough Mudder obstacles. At the Warrior Dash 5K you must safely see your way over the Deadman's Drop, the Pipeline, Mud Mounds, and Muddy Mayhem.

4. YOU CAN DRESS IN GOOFY COSTUMES.
What's a fitness event if you can't dress up in a silly costume? Superhero Scramble, out of Florida, urges its participants to "be a superhero" and dress in the costumes of their favorite superhero. It's a wonder no one ever thought of that before.

5. MOST ANYONE CAN DO IT.
Several of the obstacle course companies project tougher-than-tough images, advertising how demanding their events are and what a fierce competitor you must be to survive them. "They call us maniacs," says the promotional video for Rugged Maniac, which is owned by *Shark Tank* billionaire Mark Cuban. "We crawl through mud, jump over fire and test our physical limits. And hey, we do it just for fun."

Cuban's company and all the others offer events for all abilities, with obstacles that are good for Jane and Tarzan. The CEO and founder of Spartan is Joe De Sena, a Vermont runner who started his obstacle course series with one goal in mind: "To rip people off the couch." To this end Spartan offers training and workout programs, coaching, nutritional guidance, online education, and other assistance. Its beginning races are 3 to 5 miles long with about twenty obstacles; its toughest, the Ultra Beast, is the length of a marathon with sixty obstacles.

6. YOU CAN DO IT FOR A GOOD CAUSE.

Some obstacle course events support noteworthy causes. One is the Hard Corps series; it's run by the community services arm of the Marine Corps at Camp Pendleton in San Diego. The World Famous Mud Run, Heartbreak Ridge Run, Semper Tri, Devil Dog Duathlon, and No Beach Out of Reach 7K Run are some of its events, and the proceeds go to support programs for Marines and sailors, both active and retired, and their families.

A SHARED QUEST

ONE MORE WAY TO FIND RUNNING HAPPINESS—AND ADVENTURE

One of the recurring themes of *Running Snob* is the idea of running as a shared activity, a thing to do and have fun with others. Forget all that "loneliness of the long distance runner" stuff, as we have noted. Running is community.

Which brings us to our next subject: team running relays. Running a relay with five or seven or eleven other people (the number depends on the distance and other factors) is a terrific way to get motivated, meet and exceed your personal goals while achieving success as a group, and have a grand adventure to boot. Team relays show off some of the best qualities of running in general, as we illustrate here.

ALL TYPES OF RUNNERS, FROM BEGINNERS TO ULTRAMARATHONERS, CAN PARTICIPATE IN A TEAM RELAY AND GET A KICK OUT OF IT.

Would you ever conceive of running 200 miles across a desert or over mountains by yourself? No, of course not. That would be insane. But when you join up with a band of brothers and sisters, all united in a common cause, the craziness of the thing works to your benefit; it helps form you into a team. You're all in this insanity together.

OTHER PEOPLE, DIFFERENT TYPES OF PEOPLE, SHARE YOUR GOALS.

For a 200-mile event—200 miles is the standard distance for team relays, although there are shorter ones—you can run on a team of six people (this is an elite team) or more typically, a team of eight to twelve. Relay organizers generally recommend twelve for the common sense reason that the more runners you have, the less each person has to run. On a team of twelve for a 200-miler, each participant runs three different legs of anywhere from 3 to 9 miles apiece. The terrain and difficulty of each leg can vary greatly, so you and your teammates must choose wisely, divvying up the harder legs for the tougher, more seasoned runners.

And where do you find all these hardy souls willing to join you in your quest? Friends, family, coworkers, neighbors. If you knew them just a little bit before the relay, you are going to know them a whole lot better by the time you're all done. Guaranteed.

SNOB ASIDE

Another point to be made about team relays is that winning is hardly the foremost consideration. So much of the pleasure comes from the fellowship and camaraderie, and the feeling of having given it your very best. "Winning is nice," said Bill Bowerman, "but you savor that victory for an evening and it's gone. Competing well is just not to be equated with winning."

YOU CAN SERVE TWO SETS OF PEOPLE AS YOU RUN.

As runners so often do in marathons and other races, your team can raise money for a charity or good cause. While doing this, however, you will never forget that you are also running for another set of people: your teammates. You never want to let them down, so despite your fatigue and pain, you keep pushing down that road so you can hand the baton to the next person in the relay.

IT REPRESENTS A BIG CHALLENGE AND WILL TEST YOUR LIMITS.

You cannot just get out of bed in the morning and run a team relay that afternoon. It takes advance planning and logistical support. Besides recruiting a team, you will need drivers for the two vans that will drop off and pick up runners along the course and at least one and probably two nonrunning volunteers who will help out as needed.

A 200-miler is a two-day, one-night event, which means that you and your team will sleep somewhere out on the course during the race.

It also means that you will be running in the dark with a headlamp, flashlight, and reflective vest and clutching a cell phone in case you stray off course and get lost. (Fortunately all the relay races will walk you through the essential do's and don'ts to keep you from straying off a cliff in the middle of the night.)

IT ENDS WITH A BIG PARTY AND LOTS OF EATING AND DRINKING.

A team running relay is *not* a fun run, because in a fun run you do not go for such a long time, over such hard terrain, at such high elevations, and at such strange times of the day and night. But a team running relay does resemble a fun run in many aspects, because you're doing it with a bunch of like-minded friends, many of whom dress up in costumes and wear silly hats and fake beards and neon-pink tutus, and it all ends with a giant party, often on a beach. Additionally, a team relay gives you a chance to paint all over a couple of vans and put sayings of questionable taste ("Run Hard, Don't Suck!") on the windows, which is always entertaining.

THE SNOB 9

EPICALLY AWESOME TEAM RUNNING RELAYS

A team relay, said one organizer, is "a race, a celebration, and a vacation all wrapped up in one day of running." Because you cover so much territory, there is a sight-seeing aspect to it, both when you're running and when you're riding in the van cheering on your teammates and resting up before you take your next turn on foot.

Arranged from shorter to longer distances, here are nine race-celebration-vacations that combine hard work with spirited good fun.

PALO DURO HOT DOG 15K AND THREE-PERSON RELAY

People run this Amarillo 15K solo or in a three-person team covering about 3 miles apiece. The latter option may be preferable because the "toughest li'l road race in Texas," as it calls itself, drops 1,000 feet down into Palo Duro Canyon, the second-largest canyon in the United States after the Grand Canyon, and then climbs back out again. The running lasts one to two hours, and no van is required. But it's often, as people used to say, hot enough to fry an egg on a sidewalk, and it's an open-road course where you must keep your eye out for cars, trucks, rattlers, scorpions, spiders, skunks, and other

Texas Panhandle critters. The name derives from the free hot dogs awarded to finishers. PaloDuroHotDog.com

BEACH TO BAY RELAY MARATHON

Founded by Naval Captain John Butterfield in 1976, this Corpus Christi, Texas, 26.2-miler is held every year on Armed Forces Day and honors our nation's military. This may be the easiest marathon you will ever run because you share the load with five other people, each person on your team running 4.4 miles. No van needed. Fittingly, the course passes through the grounds of the Corpus Christi Naval Air Station before the finish on the shoreline of the Gulf Coast. BeachtoBayRelay.com

WASATCH BACK RELAY

This rugged, 188-mile overnighter in Northern Utah remains one of the most popular—and challenging—relays in the country, as it crosses three mountain passes in the Wasatch range in the northern part of the state. It's also a relay in the national Ragnar series, which includes events in Cape Cod, Chattanooga-Nashville, Las Vegas, Huntington Beach-San Diego, and other places. RagnarRelay.com

EPIC ROCKY MOUNTAIN RELAY

Epic is another relay company; it holds three overnighters in the West—one from Portland to Eugene, another in Utah and Wyoming, and this 190-miler in the Colorado Rockies. The route is definitely no flatlander; it crosses mountain passes, national forests, and "14ers," which is Colorado argot for any mountain with an elevation of 14,000 feet or above. Colorado has fifty-eight 14ers, the most of any state, and if you complete this race you will have introduced yourself to five of them. EpicRelays.com

HOOD TO COAST RELAY

The Hood to Coast is known as "the mother of all relays," and for good reason. It is the largest long-distance running relay in the world with more than a thousand teams participating. The 198-mile, two-day event is so popular it fills up every year on the first day of registration. Festivities commence at Timberline Lodge at the 6,000-foot level of Mount Hood in the Oregon interior and culminate at Seaside on the Pacific Ocean with "the largest beach party on the West Coast," say organizers. HoodCoastRelay.com

AMERICAN ODYSSEY RELAY

If you love American history—and even better, running *through* American history—this relay hits the mark. Beginning in Gettysburg, Pennsylvania, site of the epic Civil War battle and Lincoln's immortal address, it passes through two more Civil War battlegrounds—Antietam in Sharpsburg and Harpers Ferry at the confluence of the Potomac and Shenandoah Rivers—before ending, 200 miles and two days later, at the waterfront in Washington DC. We are especially fond of the race organizer's tips on how to train for the event: "Get in a van with five other smelly people, crank up the iPod and drive around for about 24 hours and then you should be ready." AmericanOdysseyRelay.com

SPOKANE TO SANDPOINT TEAM RELAY

The Spokane to Sandpoint starts at the Main Lodge on Mount Spokane in Eastern Washington and ends 200 miles later on a beach at the biggest and deepest lake in Idaho, Lake Pend Oreille. Between these two points you pass by Little Spokane River, run through downtown Spokane and along the runner's paradise known as Centennial Trail, and into northwest Idaho, all the while taking in the pleasures and sights of Big Sky Country. SpokaneToSandpoint.com

REACH THE BEACH RELAY

Mike Dionne and Rich Mazzola were two running and cycling buddies who had what was then an outlandish idea: Stage an overnight running relay in New Hampshire from the White Mountains to the Atlantic Ocean. They drove for hours and days around the state, plotting out the 201-mile course relying on a paper map (this was before GPS) and their own good instincts. The first annual Reach the Beach Relay (now also part of the Ragnar series) took place in 1999 and quickly turned into the top event of its kind in New England. Sentimentalists at heart, Dionne and Mazzola still have that crumpled old map. RTBRelay.com

SMOKY MOUNTAIN RELAY

This relay through the Smoky Mountains of North Carolina—or the Great Smokies, as they are also, and justifiably, called—draws its original inspiration from the Hood to Coast Relay, the one that started it all. It begins in a wondrous spot known as the Pink Beds, so named because of all the pink wildflowers that bloom in the spring when the race is held. As you run along the Blue Ridge Parkway and Mountain to Sea Trail, be prepared to get wet, crossing over and into streams. The finish after 214 miles is in Bryson City. SMR.SmokyMountainRelay.com

QUOTABLE SNOB

"Know yourself, so that you may live that life peculiar to you, the one and only life you were born to live. Know yourself, that you may perfect your body and find your play."

—GEORGE SHEEHAN

RUNNING SNOB QUIZ #6

YOLO RUNNING ADVENTURES

Our final Running Snob quiz is both a test and, we hope, an inspiration. It will test your knowledge of running, geography, the arts, and other matters, while supplying you with ideas on places to go and possible future running adventures. We apologize because the phrase has become terribly trite, but we're calling it our YOLO running adventure quiz. Answers follow the quiz.

1. One reporter called Le Marathon du Medoc "the world's longest, booziest race." While the first part isn't true—it is a standard marathon—the second part may be. Held in the Medoc region of France, there are more than twenty "refreshment stands" that pour red and white wine and serve oysters, cheese, steak, and ice cream to runners. The Medoc is the home of what famous French wine?
   a. Bordeaux
   b. Champagne
   c. Burgundy
   d. Chablis

2. The Empire State Building in New York City hosts the world's oldest and best known tower race. The Empire State Building Run-Up ascends 1,050 feet or 86 floors to the top of King Kong's

favorite building; the record for the distance is 9 minutes, 33 seconds. How many steps must a runner climb to reach the top?

a. an even 1,000

b. 1,576

c. 1,776, same as the date for the American Revolution

d. 1,999

3. The Motatapu is the site of one of the wildest endurance events you will find. On one day five different events—15K, marathon, ultrarun, triathlon, and mountain bike race—are held simultaneously in off-road wilderness areas that were once the hunting grounds of an indigenous people known for face and body tattoos. Where is the Motatapu located and, for bonus points, what is the name of the tribe?

a. Australia

b. Philippines

c. New Zealand

d. Burma

4. Here's another geography quiz. Mount Cranmore hosts a rugged annual mountain hill climb in which runners run two laps from the base to the top and back down with a 2,500-foot elevation gain and loss each time they do. They've held US Mountain Running championships there. Where is Mount Cranmore?

a. Colorado

b. New Hampshire

c. Vermont

d. North Carolina

5. The World Marathon Challenge consists of seven marathons on seven continents in seven days, starting in Antarctica and ending in Australia. Runners and organizers alike must cope with massive logistical challenges, including bad weather. In what month is the challenge always held to have the best possible weather conditions?

a. January

b. April

c. June

d. September

6. The Ondekoza is a phenomenal *taiko* drumming troupe that performs at major marathon festivals around the world. Its members are also religiously devoted to running. Based in Japan, the Ondekoza will accept Westerners as long as they agree to certain conditions. Which of these is a requirement for joining the troupe? (The others are not.)

    a. running a marathon

    b. living with other Ondekoza in its headquarters near Mount Fuji

    c. speaking some Japanese

    d. having drumming experience

7. Let's test your literary knowledge. The running of the bulls in Pamplona, Spain, is one of the most famous running events in the world. After they let the bulls out of a corral, people run ahead of them in the streets for about 800 meters until the animals reach a bullring. Name the 1926 Ernest Hemingway novel that first brought this risky and occasionally lethal event to the world's attention.

    a. *The Sun Also Rises*

    b. *For Whom the Bell Tolls*

    c. *Death in the Afternoon*

    d. *A Moveable Feast*

8. The London 2 Brighton Challenge is a 100k ultra that begins in London and ends at the seaside in the south of England (although you can run shorter options). Once you reach Brighton, you can visit a most unusual tourist attraction. What is it?

    a. The Brighton Eye, a big wheel (or Ferris Wheel) that is even larger than the London Eye

b. The English Channel Aquarium, where you can don a wet suit and snorkel inside a cage with more than seventy different marine species swimming around it, including sharks.

c. Coney Island Britain, a re-creation of the famous New York boardwalk transplanted to the British coast, complete with a Nathan's hot dog eating contest on the Queen's birthday.

d. The i360, the world's narrowest tower, which features a vertical cable car rising up to a glass-enclosed viewing area more than 400 feet above ground.

9. Holland, or the Netherlands, offers some of the best and *flattest* running races in Europe. The Netherlands, or Holland, also offers a gracious bounty of tulips, windmills, and good cheese. Wait a sec. What is the difference between Holland and the Netherlands, or is there one?

a. No. They are one and the same.

b. Netherlands refers to the Kingdom of the Netherlands, whereas Holland is the name of the democratic republic.

c. The Netherlands refers to all twelve provinces in the country, whereas Holland consists of only two of the provinces.

d. Holland was the original name for the country, and the Netherlands retains it for ceremonial and sentimental purposes.

10. In *Forrest Gump*, Forrest runs back and forth across the United States for years until finally, for his own reasons, he stops. The highway where he stops—known as the Forrest Gump Road—is in sight of a majestic natural landmark where many runners go to run and visit. Name the landmark.

a. Mount Rushmore

b. Niagara Falls

c. Pikes Peak

d. Monument Valley

Answers: 1. a; 2. b; 3. c., Maori; 4. b; 5. a; 6. b; 7. a; 8. d; 9. c; 10. d

ALPHABET FOR RUNNERS

Some years ago the brilliant and funny Shel Silverstein wrote a poem called "The Runners;" in it he asks, "Why does our track team run so fast/And jump with zest and zeal?" The answer lies in the illustration (also by Silverstein) that accompanies the poem. The runners run so fast because a lion is chasing after them, and they jump so far because if they don't, they will fall into a pit and impale themselves on sharp spikes at the bottom. Inspired by this poetic whimsy, here is "Alphabet for Runners," affectionately dedicated to runners everywhere.

A is for Achilles
Hero of yore
And that darn tendon
Inflamed and sore.

B is for Boston
Rodgers, Billy
Up he flew
O'er Heartbreak Hill-y.

C is for (races) Crazy
I kid you not
Grown men in diapers
And turkeys that trot.

D is for Duality
Body and mind
Running works both
At the same time.

E is for Eugene
Track Town of pluck
Everybody runs
Even the ducks.

F is for Fartlek
A Swedish bon-mot
What runners do
They fartlek—a lot!

G is for Grete (and)
Her pal Fred Lebow
They made New York
One heckuva show.

H is for the Hare
Who thought he'd won
But Turtle got 'im
In their fabled run.

I is for Inspiring
Athletes in chairs
Off they go—
With courage to spare.

J is for Joy
Child running free
In bare feet
Down by the sea.

K is for Kenyans
Ethiopians as well
Can't someone else win
Just for a spell?

L is for Liberation
"K. Switzer's" story
That was on her bib
As she ran to glory.

M is for the Mile
Miracle run
When Roger broke four
The deed was done.

N is for Night
It's dark, it's cold
Look! There's a runner
Out on the road.

O is for Olympics
Every four years
Comes soaring highs
And bitter tears.

P is for Pheidippides
"Rejoice," he cried.
"We've conquered."
Then, he died.

Q is for Quiet
Tense at the start
Poised and ready
Every beating heart.

R is for Running shorts
From first to lasss-t
You gotta have 'em
They cover the a**.

S is for Shorter
Frank-ly, the best
Won marathon gold
The ultimate test.

T is for T-shirts
Racing's prize
Sm., med., lg.
Just tell 'em your size.

U is for Ultramarathoners
Digging so deep
Miles to go
Before they sleep.

V is for Viren
Kip, Jim, Nurmi
Those who faced 'em
Sure felt squirmy.

W is for Waffle
Strange but true
How one man's breakfast
Became a shoe.

X is for 'Xhilarating
A feeling that's tops
When workout's done
Then you can stop.

Y is for Youth
Future's bright
New talent coming
Bringing their light.

Z is for Zed
Last of the pack
Shuffling in slo-mo
Way, way, way back.

ABOUT THE AUTHOR

Kevin Nelson is the author of more than twenty books, including another popular book in the Snob series, *Foodie Snob.* He has written for running publications and is the author of *The Runner's Book of Daily Inspiration,* a motivational book for runners. He lives in the San Francisco Bay Area and can be reached at his travel blog, WineTravelAdventure.com.